PERFORMANCE-BASED INSTRUCTION

Linking Training to Business Results

Dale Brethower and Karolyn Smalley

Jossey-Bass
Pfeiffer
San Francisco

Copyright © 1998 by International Society for Performance Improvement

ISBN: 0-7879-1119-4

Library of Congress Cataloging-in-Publication Data

Brethower, Dale M.

    Performance-based instruction : linking training to business
results / Dale M. Brethower and Karolyn A. Smalley.

      p.   cm.

    Includes bibliographical references and index.

    ISBN 0-7879-1119-4 (acid-free paper)

    1. Employees—Training of.   2. Transfer of training.
3. Organizational change.   4. Performance.   I. Smalley, Karolyn A.,
date. II. Title.

HF5549.5.T7B643   1998   97-45356

658.3'12404—dc21

Printed in the United States of America

Published by

350 Sansome Street, 5th Floor
San Francisco, California 94104-1342
(415) 433-1740; Fax (415) 433-0499
(800) 274-4434; Fax (800) 569-0443

Visit our website at: www.pfeiffer.com

Acquiring Editor: Larry Alexander
Marketing Manager: Matt Holt
Director of Development: Kathleen Dolan-Davies
Senior Production Editor: Dawn Kilgore
Editor: Rebecca Taff

Printing 10 9 8 7 6 5 4 3 2

 This book is printed on acid-free, recycled stock that meets or exceeds the minimum GPO and
EPA requirements for recycled paper.

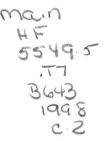
CONTENTS

v

ACKNOWLEDGMENTS

We have organized what we have learned from hundreds of people, attempting to capture the essence of their work so that others could also learn from them. We included material in the book only if it met two criteria:

1. It was based on actual work.
2. It was consistent with major research and theory in human performance technology.

The book is really a third edition; the procedures in individual chapters have been field tested in several settings and the book as a whole has been used several times in graduate courses at Western Michigan University.

There is no way we can list all the people we have learned from, but we would like to acknowledge a few individuals, alphabetically, along with the chapters that feature their work.

Michelle Bensky   Chapters One and Two
Shirley Carlyle   Chapter Ten
Aubrey Daniels   Chapter Nine
Mary Jo DeJong   Chapter One

Susan Eichkoff	Chapters Three and Five
Marcia Heiman	Chapter Thirteen
Sheldon Stone	Chapter Nine

Thank you all!

PREFACE

Performance-based instruction is both organization centered and learner centered. It improves performance of individuals and, thereby, adds value to the skill set of the learner and to the bottom line of the organization. It is only natural, then, that a book about performance-based instruction should revolve around three basic questions: "Where am I going?" "How shall I get there?" and "How will I know I've arrived?" These questions were first identified by Robert Mager (1997) in the following poem[1]:

> To rise from a zero
> To Big Campus Hero,
> To answer these questions you'll strive:
> > Where am I going,
> > How shall I get there, and
> > How will I know I've arrived?

This book is a guided tour of performance-based instruction. Each chapter is intended to provide something of value—something that can be used right away. Each chapter is also intended to contribute to the understanding of performance-based instruction: what it is, why it is valuable, and how to do it.

Chapter One is an overview that gives an example of performance-based instruction in operation. Chapters Two, Three, Four, Five, and Six provide additional examples of performance-based applications that some readers will be able to use right away. Practicing human resource development professionals are invited to ask: How can I use this tomorrow to improve the quality, efficiency, or enjoyment of my work? Readers who are not currently HRD professionals will have a greater stretch to find immediate value, but practice exercises are provided to help assess the potential value and show how to use performance-based instruction to develop self or others.

Chapter Seven begins Part Two with a comparison of performance-based instruction to the paradigms of general education and vocational education or training. People interested in big-picture issues are invited to read Chapter Seven at any time and to browse through the other chapters. It is not necessary to read in sequence; chapters were put in a sequence to fit the demands of a book, but the learner need not be bound by it. Each of the remaining chapters in Part Two shows an application that can be used to guide readers as they do similar applications, e.g., converting a course to performance-based instruction, altering existing courses to improve transfer of training, doing performance-based needs assessments, taking a systematic approach to the design of a new course, or taking some important steps toward equipping individuals with the learning skills needed in the modern workplace.

Thank you for traveling with us!

Enjoy and learn!

Karolyn Smalley   Dale Brethower
                                                                                  Ada, Michigan
                                                                                  January 1998

Note

1. Reprinted with permission from *How to Turn Learners On . . . Without Turning Them Off.* Copyright © 1997. Published by The Center for Effective Performance, 4250 Perimeter Park South, Suite 131, Atlanta, GA 30341. 1–800–558–4237.

PART ONE

A PRACTICAL APPROACH TO TRAINING ISSUES

CHAPTER ONE

PERFORMANCE-BASED INSTRUCTION: APPLICATION TO CUSTOMER SERVICE

An Overview: Where Are We Going?

Performance-based instruction uses joblike materials and procedures to help learners become capable of excellent performance. It has a specific purpose, specific benefits, and some drawbacks. Chapter One gives an example of performance-based instruction to illustrate the purpose, benefits, and drawbacks:

- *Purpose*: To add value to the performance of individuals and organizations by reducing the gap between typical (or novice) performance and excellent performance.
- *Benefit*: High ratio of benefit to cost. Development process is both systematic and efficient.
- *Drawback*: May not be suited to purposes other than improving performance.

How Shall We Get There?

An example of an application of performance-based instruction for customer service training illustrates three main features:

- *Guided Observation*: Learners experience examples or demonstrations that show why something is done, what is accomplished, and how it is accomplished.

- *Guided Practice*: Learners practice specific processes that accomplish specific results. As they practice, processes and tasks increase in difficulty, complexity, or standard of performance.
- *Demonstration of Mastery*: Learners demonstrate that they can perform the specific tasks and, thereby, generate the products or services needed in their work. Doing so enables learners and instructors to develop confidence in what learners can accomplish.

How Will We Know We've Arrived?

After analyzing the example of performance-based instruction, readers will be able to answer the following questions about performance-based instruction: What is it? What is the purpose? What are the benefits and drawbacks? How does it work? Why should I know about it?

Readers are invited to think seriously about the following questions: How could performance-based instruction similar to the example be used in other settings for other training problems? What are some examples of training projects that probably would not be suited for performance-based instruction?

A Performance-Based Example

Business Issue

The customer service department of a large company faces several ongoing problems:

- Competitive forces make improved customer service a necessity.
- Many new customer service agents (CSAs) have to be hired and brought up to speed to serve an expanding customer base. In addition, many temporary employees are used during peak seasons.
- Unless new CSAs acquire higher levels of proficiency than old CSAs, costs will rise more rapidly than the increasingly lean profit margin can support.

Performance Issues

1. The company sells a wide variety of products and a few services and uses many different sales and marketing promotions with special pricing. Both products and promotions change frequently. Most calls to CSAs involve orders already placed, e.g., "When will it arrive?" "You sent the wrong items." "You charged

the wrong price." "You are billing me, but I already sent a check." "Could I add more to my order now and receive the quantity discount?" Other calls are more general, e.g., "When does the warranty expire?" "How can I return this for repair?" "Why are your prices higher than Acme's?" "Is this item EPA approved?" "I heard you were going to bring out an updated version; if so, when?" Customer service agents are supposed to handle customer questions, find answers, and sell additional products.

2. Long-term CSAs have acquired misinformation and bad habits, which they pass on to customers and new agents.

3. Long-term customers have specific and sometimes erroneous expectations about the customer support services available; new customers have little notion of what is available or how to describe the services they need.

4. The training programs already in place are long and costly to operate, very difficult to keep updated, and cannot be delivered on a timely basis.

The human resource development (HRD) department has developed a performance-based training system to respond to these business and performance challenges.

Guided Observation

The new performance-based training program for CSAs begins with a tour of the work area. They see thirty people, each talking on the telephone in a small work station. They stop to listen to people working with customers, guided by a checklist that shows the steps and standards for:

1. Answering the telephone,
2. Listening to the customer,
3. Analyzing the customer's situation,
4. Identifying alternatives,
5. Taking action, and
6. Probing to determine whether the customer is satisfied.

As trainees listen, they take notes about how the CSAs meet the criteria on the checklist. At the end of the tour, trainees meet with two experienced CSAs and ask questions about what the CSAs accomplish for the company, their most enjoyable and most frustrating experiences with customers, etc. When they finish talking with CSAs, the trainees move into a training room that contains several work stations similar to those they have just seen.

Working in groups of three, they discuss what they have observed and write a mission statement that describes the importance of the job and the major tasks and responsibilities. They then compare their mission statements with the official one that was developed by the customer service representatives themselves and approved by management. They next move to work stations to practice the process they observed.

Guided Practice

One trainee works from a script, playing the role of a customer. The second trainee takes the role of a customer service agent, working from an information sheet that contains the material needed to deal with the customers' issues. The third trainee observes the interaction, using the same checklist that was used during the tour. After the practice phone call is completed, the observer comments on the process, then goes to a simulated work station and answers the telephone to take a similar call. The second trainee, working from a script and sitting behind a partition, plays the customer. The practice calls are examples of calls routinely dealt with by customer service agents. Several rounds of calls are practiced.

Demonstration of Mastery

Handling the calls well demonstrates mastery of the material; handling the calls improperly shows that the trainee needs more practice. Trainees practice until they pass all the performance tests by handling simulated calls well. The simulated work station is then plugged into the live customer service line. As the trainee takes calls, the trainer uses the checklist to observe and certify that the trainee is ready to perform the job.

Analysis of Example

1. Does performance-based instruction always work like the example?

Not always. As the HRD department developed the performance-based training, it was easy to establish the guided observation and to do guided practice so that novice customer service agents could master very simple calls. Although many calls are simple, many are complex. Bringing people up to speed with complex calls might involve different tactics. Several different ways could be used, depending on the complexity of the knowledge required, the amount of knowledge that could be made available through job aids or electronic performance support systems, the importance of the job, the amount of lead time for development, and the ingenuity of the HRD staff. Here are some best-case, worst-case, and in-between scenarios.

- *Worst-Case Scenario*: In a worst-case scenario, trainees would be given a section from a complex and confusing manual and told to learn it. After a time, they would go to the simulated work station to take calls that had been scripted to require knowledge of the section of the manual just studied.
- *Best-Case Scenario*: A best-case scenario would involve the trainees doing all their learning at the simulated work station, taking progressively more demanding calls. The scenario would be possible if there had been adequate lead time, budget, and design team competence to build an electronic performance support system (Gery, 1991) that could quickly provide the trainee with the information needed to answer calls. (Note, however, that even with adequate lead time, the cost and competence requirements for design of such a system would put it beyond many budgets; complex electronic support systems are cutting-edge, rather than state-of-the-art.)
- *In-Between Scenarios*: Other scenarios would fall between the best case and the worst case. For example, trainees might be given specially designed manuals, information sheets, and other job aids instead of the sort of manual that is hard for mere mortals to understand (Harless, 1980; Horn, 1976; Lineberry & Bullock, 1980). Practice exercises might be designed in which small groups of trainees worked together; each person in the group would specialize in one or more types of information, so that several trainees would play the role of one customer service agent in responding to a set of questions that might be asked by customers. The trainees might add specialties until each trainee could handle most or all calls.

2. What do the scenarios have in common?

In all three scenarios, the knowledge required to do the job is learned in the context of the job. The training exercises, support materials, and all the performance tests are as joblike as time, budget, and ingenuity allow.

3. Does using a job context take more time?

A performance-based approach actually minimizes learning time. Although it would be faster to store all the information in learners' heads during one phase of training and then have them learn to talk to customers in another phase, it does not work that way. Detailed information has a way of becoming mixed or muddled or disappearing entirely between "storage" and "practice"; performance-based instruction links the acquisition of knowledge to its utilization. It is more efficient because it prevents any slippage by using concrete examples and immediate application and practice.

4. What is the purpose of performance-based instruction?

Performance-based instruction has a narrowly defined purpose: reducing the gap between novice and competent performance (or the gap between typical and excellent performance). Performance-based instruction is designed to enable people to bridge the gap between their initial knowledge, skills, and attitudes (KSA) and the KSA they need to perform well on the job. For example, the customer service agent must deal with a very wide range of customer questions, concerns, and complaints. Product knowledge, company policy, etc., are taught in performance-based instruction, but not separately. They are taught in the context of answering the specific questions customers ask. The purpose is to bring customer service agents up to speed so that they can serve customers well, not teach them to recite policies or product information.

5. What are the benefits?

Performance-based instruction enables trainees to achieve high levels of performance quickly. Their energies are channeled into learning just what they need to perform the job well, not irrelevant, nice-to-know, or tangential material. The narrowly defined purpose is as important to the learner as style and function are to someone buying clothing. One size does not fit all and one coat does not function well in all climates and seasons. Similarly, teaching people everything that could ever be needed does not fit the learning process and, therefore, does not equip learners to deal with all potential situations. However, there are drawbacks and benefits to both well-tailored special-purpose clothing and to performance-based instruction.

6. What are the drawbacks?

The narrow focus on performance can be a drawback because much general or nice-to-know material is not included or is included only in reference materials. What happens if something new or unexpected comes up? What if the reasons for doing something are important? Will people be able to learn more on their own?

These are legitimate questions; developers or users of performance-based instruction should understand the drawbacks and face, head-on, the tension between specific relevance on one hand and breadth of coverage on the other. The design challenge is to teach specifics, but to be sure that the specifics become stepping stones to the broader knowledge, flexibility, and adaptability of performance needed over time. Some specific instances given in later chapters will show how performance-based instruction enables the general knowledge to emerge from an array of specific examples.

7. What is the process?

Figure 1.1 illustrates the process for developing performance-based instruction that was used by the HRD group in the earlier example. It begins with identifying a business need, a gap between current and desired performance.

8. Does it always work that way?

It is a judgment call about how carefully to do, document, and involve others in each phase. It is always a good idea to take a few minutes to think through the

FIGURE 1.1. DEVELOPING PERFORMANCE-BASED INSTRUCTION.

Project Phase	Key Questions	Sample Answers
Specification of Business Need	Why train? What is the strategic or current business need for performance improvement?	Our customer service is good, but we have a severe problem in bringing new people up to speed quickly. We are losing sales opportunities.
Specification of Performance Requirements	What performance products are needed? What standards? What performance support?	Promptly answered calls that leave the customer with useful information and satisfied with the service. We should establish clear feedback from customers and management to customer service people.
Design Phase One: Specification of Work Processes	How can people do it? What processes can people use to produce the products? How will we guide practice?	We'll develop a checklist to show the procedures and guide practice.
Design Phase Two: Specification of Instructional Processes	Does the overall design link learners and workplace? Does each unit?	Yes. People will practice simulated tasks for each unit. The final tasks will simulate actual work conditions.
Implementation and Evaluation	Are analysis and design done properly? Do the design and implementation reflect principles of adult learning and performance? Do they actually work?	Yes. We followed the design process well: we identified a business need, the performance required, the standards, and the process. When we implemented, we saw that the active involvement and immediate application of relevant material supported adult learning. People performed well on the job.

entire process; sometimes the first two phases are just guesswork. Sometimes the evaluation is also guesswork. Fortunately, after a course has been used a time or two, many of the unknowns are known and skillful designers can complete the process competently.

How Performance-Based Instruction Works

The customer service training scenarios illustrate how performance-based instruction works:

* Learners are oriented through *guided observation*.
* They learn to do what they have observed through *guided practice*.
* They demonstrate *mastery* before being turned loose on the job.

There are several important points about how performance-based instruction works that are not obvious from the customer service example given earlier. In fact, some of the nuances won't be obvious until several examples are worked through in later chapters.

Guided Observation

Intelligent adults and most children want to know at least three things when we offer to instruct them: *why* something is worth doing, *what* it accomplishes, and *how* to do it. Guided observation answers all three questions. The guided observation in the customer service example showed learners *why* they needed to learn the material, i.e., that customers ask all sorts of things and that the life of the customer service agent is more pleasant when he or she has the answers. The observation checklist shows *what* the customer service agent accomplishes at various stages in handling a customer call and provides specific guidance about *how* to do it. The guided tour helps to answer a key question for the learner: "Why is this material important to me and to the employer?"

When trainees complete the tour and ask an experienced customer service agent about enjoyable and frustrating experiences with customers, they can also be primed to ask follow-up questions: "What happens if you give a customer the wrong information?" "Why does the company hire so many customer service agents; how does this job help the company?" "How does the company know that this job is worth doing?" "Is it hard to put on a 'company face'?" "If a lot of customers have the same question, shouldn't we tell somebody so they can fix the flaws in our products or systems? Why do you bother to do a good job, as opposed to doing just enough to get by?" "Do you think your supervisors really care whether or not you do a good job?"

The trainees can also be encouraged to question other workers and to question supervisors whenever they have the opportunity. Although it is not always wise to ask them, adults do have questions and, under the right circumstances, they will ask them. Finding out the answers can be very motivating for the learner. For the questioning opportunities alone, a tour and meeting people who are doing the job are worth a great deal.

Structuring the tour by providing observation checklists, sample questions, and permission to ask them involves the learners immediately and meaningfully in learning. By the end of the tour, the new customer service agents have a reasonably clear answer to "Why?" and an overview of "What must we learn in order to perform the way these expert customer service agents perform?" and "How do they do it?" The tour prepares novices for the guided practice and shows them what mastery is. The guided practice enables them to perform as they have observed the expert customer service agents performing. This technique, of course, can be used to teach other types of performance.

Guided Practice

After the tour the novice customer service agents begin guided practice exercises. In the worst-case scenario the guidance would come from studying portions of the reference material and practicing that material with simulated calls. Much of the learning would occur during the practice calls, although obviously some things are learned from reading the manuals. In the best-case and intermediate scenarios, most of the learners' time would be spent working through guided practice activities.

Figure 1.2 shows the structure of a guided practice session for the CSAs. Each call has the same basic pattern. There is input from the customer, which the customer service agent processes and then provides a response. Each call has the same basic pattern, although a complex call would require several rounds of determining needs and providing information. It qualifies as guided practice because there is time to look things up, if necessary. In the best case, the needed information would be easy to obtain through an electronic support system or other well-designed job aid or documentation. The practice sessions would move quickly and fluidly from one call to the next, the customer service agent learning by doing. In the worst case, the trainee could listen to two or three calls to determine the general kinds of information needed, go "off line" for a while to study, then come back "on line" to finish and thereby show mastery.

FIGURE 1.2. THE STRUCTURE OF A GUIDED PRACTICE SESSION.

Input from Customer	Process	Response to the Customer
Call	Greet customer, determine need. Search documentation, if necessary, to obtain information.	Provide information to customer. Check to determine whether information satisfies customer.
Customer indicates need	Determine need. Search documentation if necessary.	Provide information to customer. Check to determine whether information satisfies customer.
Customer indicates satisfaction	Record transactions.	Thank customer.

Demonstrations of Mastery

The novice customer service agents demonstrate mastery frequently during the training. In the worst-case scenario they would study specific parts of manuals and other reference documents and then do a role-play exercise at a simulated work station to demonstrate mastery of that segment of material. Mastery would still be tested by performing in the context of the job, i.e., responding to common customer questions and concerns. Each role play would be practice if they stumbled and a demonstration of mastery if they did it well.

Demonstrations of mastery occur within guided practice sessions. In the worst-case scenario, the mastery demonstrations would occur during short periods "on line" separated by obvious chunks "off line." In the best-case scenario, the demonstrations of mastery would occur during each guided practice episode. Each demonstration of mastery would be a little victory that maintained the learner's momentum and motivation.

In the best-case scenario, the little victories would be frequent because practice and demonstrations of mastery would be seamlessly interwoven during the training sessions. Think of it this way: in the worst-case scenario, there would be a lot of "studying" and then a demonstration of mastery; in the best-case scenario, there would be very small amounts of "studying" during the practice session.

In both the best-case and worst-case scenarios, the little victories for each demonstration of mastery would be consolidated into a final demonstration of mastery that would occur when the simulated work station was plugged in so that the new customer service agents took real calls. An instructor/coach would be available to help if they stumbled or to certify mastery if they handled calls well.

It is also possible to have simulated calls routed to the work station. A role player would work from a script that tested mastery of specific areas that were critical but infrequent. The role plays would assure opportunities to demonstrate mastery of material that might not come up for some time in actual practice. It is important both to the trainee and to the employer that everyone demonstrate mastery of difficult as well as routine calls. Careful use of role playing can assure quality and integrity of testing without violating customer or employee rights to privacy.

Experienced customer service agents take delight in describing critical incidents that work well for this purpose. Here are some possible critical incidents from actual call centers. How would you deal with:

- A call from a very persistent person who claims to have connections with people in high places in the company or government
- A bomb threat
- A despondent customer who says that receiving a defective product is the "last straw," causing him/her to contemplate suicide
- A frightened latch-key child who inexplicably calls the support service number rather than 911 while someone is trying to break into his or her apartment
- An unethical purchasing agent for a major competitor testing the responsiveness of customer support
- An angry person who thinks he/she has called a competitor

After demonstrating mastery on a few very difficult calls, a customer service agent can approach the real work station with butterflies rather than anxiety. The first few calls will seem easy in comparison with the training and build confidence. The transition will be even smoother if the training program includes a coach who is available to trainees during their first hours on the job.

A Caveat

Best Case Is Sometimes Worst Case and Vice Versa

The guided practice exercises are the most costly part of performance-based instruction in terms of design time and trainee time. In the worst-case scenario earlier, little design time had been done, so the major cost would be trainee time. With an expensive designer, a rather simple job, few trainees, and a low cost of error on the job, the worst case would make economic sense and, in fact, may be the best case, i.e., the worst case from the learning perspective can be the best case from an economic perspective.

But if the cost of error were high, there were many trainees, or the job were complex, the cost of learning time and/or the cost of errors would provide economic justification for extensive design and development work on the guided practice portion of the training. The best-case example given earlier was only best because many customer service jobs are complex, cost of errors is high, and there are a substantial number of trainees, from turnover as well as the fact that the content of these jobs changes frequently and that changes occur in products, services, policies, customer expectations, etc. It is the best case as a rule, but there are exceptions.

CHAPTER TWO

PERFORMANCE-BASED INSTRUCTION ON THE JOB

An Overview

Where Are We Going?

The focus of this chapter is on-the-job training (OJT)[1]: *why* it is important, *what* it is, and *how* to do it.

- *Purpose*: Performance-based OJT enables people to get up to speed quickly on a new job or on new procedures or tasks. In addition, procedures are documented to make it easier to implement changes or to train additional people later.
- *Benefits*: Because it is so common, more money is spent on OJT than any other form of training; because most of it is unplanned, much of the cost is not monitored and quality is not assured. On the other hand, there are practical procedures that could improve both the quality and cost-effectiveness of OJT.
- *Drawbacks*: There is enormous room for improvement in OJT. It typically occurs by default. In large organizations the HRD department may lack the time, mandate, or resources to manage OJT effectively. Many small organizations have no HRD professionals. Improving OJT is, therefore, a monumental task with monumental potential.

How Shall We Get There?

First, we will review an example of performance-based OJT to see how it can be used in a specific setting. Then, we will analyze the example to understand why things were done the way they were and see how it works so that we can use it in other settings.

- *Guided Observation*: Learners experience examples that show why key tasks are done, what is accomplished by each task, and how each task is done. Special attention is given to products or results: People learn to identify characteristics of good versus poor products or results and good versus poor processes for doing the tasks.
- *Guided Practice*: Learners practice doing tasks that accomplish real work. As they practice, they need less guidance and improve both in quality and efficiency of performance.
- *Demonstrations of Mastery*: Learners demonstrate to themselves and others that they can perform the specific tasks and the job as a whole in accordance with established standards.

Finally, we will consider some caveats and select from an array of practice exercises to start doing performance-based OJT.

How Will We Know We've Arrived?

Readers are invited to use the following self-assessment checklist:

Self-Assessment Checklist

- Do I know of several situations in which I could—or believe others should—use performance-based OJT?
- Can I identify or describe what makes performance-based OJT valuable and feasible in some of those situations?
- Can I list the actions I would need to take beforehand to prepare the workplace, the trainer, and the trainee for OJT?
- Can I identify what trainees should observe during guided observation?
- Can I find ways to assure that coaching and feedback are provided to guide practice effectively?
- Can I identify ways for trainees to demonstrate mastery?

Being able to answer these questions demonstrates an understanding of performance-based OJT.

Readers are also invited to take on some performance-based OJT projects, using suggestions provided at the end of the chapter to guide and evaluate the work. Those who are already in a workplace that supports OJT are invited to do several projects to become really expert.

Performance-Based Example

Guided Observation

New employees of a shopping service begin their training by observing an experienced employee going through a supermarket to fill an order. The experienced employee begins the demonstration by showing the trainees the order to be filled and saying, "When we finish with this order, I want you to tell me whether I've done a good job—and I'll ask you for suggestions about how I could do it better. Please ask at least two questions before we start."

A trainee might ask, "How can I tell if you are doing a good job before I even know how to do it myself?" and the trainer might reply, "Let's make a list of what good performance is. What do our customers want? What does this store want from us? What do we have to do to make enough money to pay our wages?" After some discussion, the new employee would have a checklist of performance criteria such as accuracy of filing the order, speed of completing it, and courtesy to other shoppers. The trainer might then say, "OK. Now watch me and tell me how well I do! Ask questions as we go." After the order is filled, the trainer might say, "How did I do?" and the trainee and the trainer would discuss the process.

For the next order, the trainer might say, "This time, I want you to tell me exactly what to do to fill this order. If you are stuck, ask questions. If you tell me to do something the wrong way, I'll do it that way unless that would cause a big problem for a customer."

Guided Practice

After a few orders have been filled in this way, the trainer might say, "You seem to know what to do. This time, you fill the order. I won't say anything unless you are about to do something dangerous. When you finish, we'll talk about how well you did and see if we can figure out how to do the next order even better." After a few orders have been filled, the trainer and the trainee will have evolved tactics for filling orders effectively and well, e.g., preplanning a route through the store, filling two or three orders at once.

Demonstration of Mastery

The trainer might then say, "Here are two large orders. I'll do one and you do the other. We'll meet at the check-out stand and double check one another's work." In addition, the trainer would review any documentation produced by the trainee (e.g., procedure descriptions or criterion checklists) to assure that they were accurate guides to high-quality performance.

Analysis of the OJT Example

1. Why does the trainee evaluate the performance of the trainer?

The goal is for the employee to learn "good" performance, i.e., value-added performance that meets company standards. Knowing what the standards are and knowing why the standards have to be what they are enable the trainee to evaluate various ways of doing the job and use his or her head as well as hands during the learning process. Starting with evaluation keeps the purpose of the job or task in focus. In short, it makes learning easier.

In addition, the trainer is modeling a very important attitude: being open to feedback about performance. This sets the tone for the trainer to provide feedback about trainee performance.

2. Why not give the trainee the checklist of criteria?

The simplest answer is that, for many tasks and many jobs, the checklist does not exist until the trainer and trainee make it. If one exists, it can be used or it could be designed beforehand, but it is often more effective to design it on the spot. Anyone qualified to do the training, i.e., anyone who knows the difference between good and bad performance and who can demonstrate good performance, can serve as a model for the checklist. (By making the checklist, the trainee demonstrates understanding of the task.) Even when a checklist already exists, it is best to discuss it, e.g., by pointing to a criterion and asking, "What's your best guess about why we have that criterion?" Asking the question indicates that the trainee's ideas will be respected and also provides a chance for him or her to think about the task.

3. How does this work for a really complicated job?

The procedure is the same:

1. Begin with evaluation of performance, continuing until the steps in the process and criteria for good products are clarified.
2. Have the trainee "coach" the trainer through the steps, including evaluating the product or result to ensure that it is "good."

3. Have the trainer coach trainee through the performance.
4. Have the trainee practice, with coaching, until performance is good.
5. End the formal OJT with a demonstration of mastery.
6. Keep monitoring quality of performance on the job.
7. Continue coaching as needed.

The shopper's job is really quite complicated, as the trainee will discover. For example, the trainee must learn what to do when:

- An item is out of stock
- A comparable item is on sale (would the customer want a specific brand or a lower price?)
- The store is crowded
- Other customers notice that the shopper is familiar with the store and interrupt for locations of specific items
- The shopper and another customer approach the check-out stand at the same time, etc.

Many simple tasks make up a truly complex job; the procedure can be used for one task at a time for other parts of the shopper's job, such as planning the delivery route, avoiding traffic and road construction, and obtaining feedback from customers.

4. When is performance-based OJT used?
Whenever:

- Someone begins a new job
- There are significant changes in the tasks that constitute a job
- There are significant changes in the ways the tasks are performed
- Cross-training is desired

5. Why wasn't an analysis done before this training was designed?
Undoubtedly the person doing the training analyzed it and refined the procedures by trial and error on the job. This process is summarized in Figure 2.1.

How Performance-Based OJT Works

Guided Observation

Guided observation enables the trainee to learn, through observation and discussion of real work tasks, the *why, what,* and *how* of excellent performance.

FIGURE 2.1. DEVELOPING PERFORMANCE-BASED INSTRUCTION.

Project Phase	Key Questions	Sample Answers
Specification of Business Need	What is the strategic or current business need for performance improvement?	Most of our employees are part time and there is high turnover. That slows down the growth of the company; however, we can't afford to pay more or change the nature of the work.
Specification of Performance Requirements	What performance products are needed? What standards? What performance support?	Shopping baskets filled quickly and accurately. The supervisor coaches during training but after that there's little support. We should change that.
Design Phase One: Specification of Work Processes	How can people do it? What processes can people use to produce the products? How will we guide practice?	We'll model the performance to show people how it can be done. We'll have learners coach the coach so we're sure they understand; then we'll coach as they practice.
Design Phase Two: Specification of Instructional Processes	How does the overall design link learners and workplace? How does each unit?	Learners work filling actual orders. As they become proficient, the coach does less coaching and has them do it on their own. Then they are at work!
Implementation and Evaluation	Are analysis and design done properly? Do the design and implementation reflect principles of adult learning and performance? Do they actually work?	Yes, we followed the design process well: We identified a business need, the performance required, the standards, and the modeled the process. Learners did real work, practicing until they could do it well. They did better than employees who'd been there longer but weren't as well trained.

In the case of the shopper, the *why* relates to the nature of the business: the shopper must shop in a way that the customer values and in a way that enables the shopping company to make money.

The *what* relates to the specifics of *what* the work accomplishes for the customer (and the company): *What* is accomplished? *What* includes the criteria for good performance—the standards for timeliness, quality, and cost. Shopping results in goods ready to be delivered to the customer. This adds value only if it meets specific criteria: customers want specific things at a specific time and at a specific price; the shopper must shop quickly and accurately enough so that the company can make money by providing the service.

The *how* relates to the several possible ways to do a task so that it meets performance standards. People learn how something is done but do not yet develop skill in actually doing it.

Learning the *why, what, and how* takes both observation and discussion. For example, the trainee will not be able to observe the cumulative impact of his or her performance on customers and on the company bottom line. But unless the trainee knows, at least in a general way, how performance impacts the customer and the bottom line, he or she cannot perform intelligently and can only perform in a monkey-see, monkey-do way.

Guided Practice

Guided observation sets the stage for effective practice. The trainee practices the task or job in a way that meets company standards and helps to serve customers. The *why* and *what* are clear and guide the practice so that the trainee can learn *how*. As the shopper trainee completes each order, performance is discussed:

- What was done well?
- What was not done well enough?
- How can it be done better next time?

Such discussions set the stage for the next round of practice. Without them (and without coaching during the performance), the practice would not be guided effectively; learning would be slow at best.

In the case of really complex tasks or jobs, guided practice must take place over long periods of time, sometimes called internships or apprenticeships.

Demonstration of Mastery

Mastery criteria should be as high as the workplace demands and as high as the trainer's skill allows. If the trainer is skilled at coaching, the trainee can aspire to and attain high standards with diligent practice and a minimum of frustration; high standards are more fun to achieve and yield better value for the organization and the employee. If there are several tasks involved in a job, each task should be practiced until mastery is automatic. There should be additional practice in situations that demand completion of several tasks.

Tips and Caveats

1. Expert performers tend to do tasks quickly and take shortcuts that would be risky for a novice; it is difficult for them to slow down enough to demonstrate their process or to be coached by trainees. They require practice before becoming good demonstrators or trainers. It is desirable to demonstrate by doing a task very quickly once, then a second time slowly, explaining to the trainee that the first showed mastery and the second was slower to make it easier to see.

2. The ability to break complex tasks into simpler tasks that can be demonstrated readily is, itself, a complex skill set that not all experts and not all trainers master readily. One solution is to have teams analyze complex tasks; another is to have an HRD professional who has learned the analysis skills assist other OJT trainers.

3. It is often a good idea to begin OJT by using the process to teach safety, troubleshooting, or error-correction procedures before teaching the main procedures. The rationale for safety first is obvious; teaching troubleshooting procedures and error-correction procedures first helps teach *why* the basic procedures are done the way they are.

4. Some people thought to be proficient at key tasks will, in fact, not be proficient and would teach poor procedures or low standards of performance. That is one reason to have trainees produce documentation. Having several people who perform the job check the documentation helps prevent or correct this problem.

5. Trainees sometimes reach proficiency quickly and outperform people who have been on the job for some time. That can have unpleasant side effects. One way to prevent the problem is to promote an atmosphere of continuous improvement, in which learning from one another is expected; another way is to have the entire team function as "coach" and reward the entire team when the trainee performs well.

6. Performance is both an activity and a product or result of the activity. Trainees must learn, during guided observation, to identify differences between good products or results and not-so-good products and results. Discriminating good from not-so-good supports guided practice and sets standards for mastery.

Practice Exercises

Becoming good at design, implementation, and maintenance of performance-based OJT requires practice. Much, if not all, of the practice can occur on the job. Some suggested practice exercises are given below. The authors strongly recommend those marked with an asterisk.

Guided Observation Exercise One

1. Observe, if possible, as someone else does OJT. Describe the procedure the trainer uses. Describe what worked well. Describe what worked less well.
2. Compare the OJT you observed with performance-based OJT. How is performance-based OJT similar to what you observed? How is it different?
3. Figure out what you learned from the observation, analysis, and comparison. What are some things you want to avoid or be sure to do?
4. Begin drafting some of your own performance standards for doing performance-based OJT. You might want to develop standards for guided observation, guided practice, and demonstrations of mastery.

Guided Observation Exercise Two

OJT happens every time someone starts a new job. For every million OJT activities, how many would you guess are done competently? No one knows, but here is a way to estimate. Interview about ten people by asking: "When you first started your current job, how did you learn to do it well?"

1. If you find someone who describes a highly effective OJT process, celebrate and try to find out how it happened.
2. If none of the ten describes highly effective OJT, interview another ten. Keep going until you have a large enough sample to make a wild but reasonable guess about whether it is 1 in 10, 1 in 100, 1 in 1,000, or 1 in a million. (Our guess is that it is less than 1 in 10 and more than 1 in a million, maybe around 1 in 1,000.)

Guided Practice Exercise One*

Learn how to do a specific task, perhaps a part of someone else's job or perhaps doing part of your work in a more effective way.

1. Use the worksheet for self-guided OJT, Figure 2.2. Ask the questions on the worksheet to find where you are going, how you will get there, and how you will know when you have arrived.
2. As you discover the answers, practice doing the task. Practice until you achieve the level of mastery you desire. Sometimes, just being able to do it accurately is enough, at first, because you will have plenty of practice on the job to reach high standards or fluency.

FIGURE 2.2. WORKSHEET FOR SELF-GUIDED OJT: LEARNING SPECIFIC TASKS.

Questions	Notes
Guided Observation: *Why? What? How?* What is the work product? (or result? or service?)	
Why is doing it right important? (How does it benefit the customer? make things easier?)	
May I see an example of a good one? May I see one that's not quite good enough?	
How can I tell the difference between a good one (product or service or result) and one that's not good enough?	
Would you show me how to do it? Have I described it correctly? (After watching, describe the process, revising until you can describe it accurately.)	
Let me see if I understand it. Would you do it slowly and let me tell you what's next?	
Guided Practice: *How shall I get there?* May I try it now? Please warn me if I'm about to do something terrible!	
What did I do right? What should I do to do it better next time?	
Mastery: *How will I know I've arrived?* What are the actual standards or criteria for good performance?	
Am I meeting the standards? (Are my products good enough? Am I doing it quickly enough?)	

Guided Practice Exercise Two*

Design, implement, and evaluate an OJT procedure for a specific task for someone else to learn. Find a task that is real, worthwhile, and simple. Filling out a form, answering the telephone properly, signing on to the Internet, performing the trial close for a sales period, setting a table, taking a meal order from a table of ten people, using e-mail, printing an envelope on the laser printer, sending a delayed fax, etc., are some ideas.

1. Use the checklist in Figure 2.3 as you complete the major steps in a performance-based OJT procedure. Use the checklist as is or tailor it to the OJT project you do.
2. If the task is simple, check off the steps as a debriefing after the OJT episode. Doing the OJT procedure generates documentation of some of the steps, of course, but the checklist might be a useful reminder and help summarize the exercise for you and/or the trainee.

Demonstration of Mastery

Keep a record of the OJT projects you complete and checklists, monitoring forms, etc., that you produce. These documents will help you remember what you have accomplished, provide data to show progress, and allow you to improve the procedures you use.

As you practice performance-based OJT and observe others, refine your standards and practice until you are proficient.

Note

1. Estimates of employer investment in workplace training hover around $210 billion annually. About $30 billion, or 1 to 2 percent of employers' payrolls, is estimated to be spent on formal training, while another $180 billion is invested in informal or on-the-job, training. (A.P. Carnevale, L.J. Gainer, & J. Villet. *Training in America: The Organization and Strategic Role of Training.* San Francisco: Jossey-Bass, 1990, p. 23.) Also, *Training Magazine* estimates that the cost of formal training in 1996 was close to $60 billion. The estimate is based on budgets for companies with one hundred or more employees, so it undoubtedly is understated. If the estimated 6 to 1 ratio of budgeted training to OJT is accurate, the OJT price tag is probably well beyond $300 billion.

FIGURE 2.3. SAMPLE CHECKLIST FOR COMPLETING EACH STEP IN PERFORMANCE-BASED OJT.

Guided Observation	Trainee	Trainer
The knowledge step is complete when the trainee has produced documentation that answers these questions:		
• What are the products of the task?		
• Why are the products important?		
• What are the differences between good and bad products?		
• How is the task performed?		
The coaching step of the guided observation phase is complete when the trainee can coach the trainer through the task so that the trainer does it accurately, producing a good product or result.		
Guided Practice		
Coaching to Accuracy: The first step in guided practice is to enable the trainee to do the task accurately. The step is complete when the trainee can do the task successfully without coaching.		
Practice to Proficiency: The second step in guided practice is to enable the trainee to do the task to a high standard of performance. The step is complete when the trainee can perform the task with speed and accuracy, essentially without thinking about it.		
Demonstration of Mastery		
Mastery is demonstrated at least three times in performance-based OJT: 1. During guided practice (typically monitored by the trainer/coach)		
2. At the beginning of work on-the-job (typically monitored by both the trainer and the trainee's supervisor and/or peers)		
3. On the job (monitored by the worker and the supervisor and/or peers)		

PERFORMANCE-BASED TEAMWORK TRAINING

An Overview

Where Are We Going?

Chapter Three focuses on designing instruction that improves teamwork: *why* teamwork training is important, *what* performance-based teamwork training is, and *how* to do it.

- *Purpose*: The purpose of performance-based teamwork training is to enable individuals to learn how to work as a team to solve problems and to improve their teamwork skills.
- *Benefits*: As the pace of change increases, so too does the need for coordinated action based on technological, marketplace, and financial knowledge. So much knowledge is needed that one person cannot acquire it all, and increasingly work is done in cooperation with others, often in explicit teams to achieve common objectives. However, there is enormous room for improvement in teamwork. People must pool their knowledge as well as their energies. Helping people to be valuable team members is increasingly important to the success of HRD professionals. Organizations and individuals who learn how to pool knowledge and energy by working in teams have a distinct advantage over those who do not. Teamwork is no longer an option, but essential to success.

- *Drawbacks*: Especially in Western societies, great social value has been placed on individual effort. The people who rise to the top of a large organization do so, in part, because they compete effectively with their peers. Retaining individual initiative while practicing teamwork is easy. Establishing and supporting teamwork requires changes in organizational processes, reporting relationships, reward structures, and long-standing habits.

How Shall We Get There?

First, we will look at an example that illustrates the teamwork training process.

Second, we will analyze the example to understand why things were done as they were.

Third, we will look at the key elements to see how they could be applied in other settings. We will discover that the process involves guided observation, guided practice, and demonstration of mastery.

- *Guided Observation*: Learners learn through experience examples or demonstrations that show what tasks are and are not appropriate for teams, what key tasks are necessary for workplace teamwork, why key tasks are necessary, what is accomplished by each task, how each task is accomplished, and by whom.
- *Guided Practice*: Learners practice doing real tasks that accomplish real work. As they practice, they master increasing numbers of team skills, need less guidance, and improve both quality and fluency of performance.
- *Demonstrations of Mastery*: Learners demonstrate that they can perform the specific tasks and in accordance with high standards.

Finally, we will consider some tips and caveats and select from an array of practice exercises.

How Will We Know We've Arrived?

Readers are invited to use the self-assessment questions interspersed throughout the chapter as well as the following self-assessment checklist. An alternate version of the checklist can be found at the end of the chapter.

Self-Assessment Checklist

- Are there situations in my workplace that would benefit from the use of problem solving as the vehicle for teamwork?

- Am I able to assign problem-solving tasks to team members so that tasks get done and teamwork skills are learned?
- Am I able to use Figure 3.1 to help people learn to do problem-solving tasks?
- Am I able to use Figure 3.2 to help people learn the team member responsibilities and roles?
- Can I modify the tools (Figures 3.1 and 3.2) to match other terminology being used in my workplace?
- Can I develop one or two sample agendas for team meetings?
- Can I provide a plausible rationale for each of the main problem-solving steps and team roles in language that would be understood in my workplace?

Readers may also do the guided practice exercises at the end of the chapter to discover whether performance-based teamwork training might be useful for them.

Readers may wish to design and do several additional projects to practice the skills of using performance-based instruction to enable their teams to function effectively. Several rounds of practice will help them acquire more and more of the complex skills required to cope with difficult problems, e.g., team building within top management teams that have a history of in-fighting.

Performance-Based Team Building Example

The example is of teamwork training in a small high-tech company (150 employees, $12 million in sales). The company does rapid prototyping work for Fortune 100 clients. Figure 3.1 summarizes the procedure that was used to decide that teamwork training was cost effective and would provide an immediate return on investment.

Guided Observation

The teamwork training begins with discussions of examples of production problems and production successes that have occurred in recent months. The group as a whole (a production supervisor, production scheduler, quality technician, maintenance person, customer service specialist, and a human resource specialist) identifies three successes and three failures. After listing these, the trainer asks group members (they are not a team yet) to identify instances in which good teamwork contributed to the successes and poor teamwork contributed to the failures. Each

FIGURE 3.1. TEAMWORK AND PROBLEM-SOLVING TRAINING.

Project Phase	Key Questions	Sample Answers
Specification of Business Need	What is the strategic or current business need for performance improvement?	Our work is constantly changing. Our competitive edge is time; we do things faster than any of our competitors. To maintain that edge we must continuously improve. We believe that requires teamwork at every level.
Specification of Performance Requirements	What performance products are needed? What standards? What performance support?	We must solve current problems and implement technological innovations. The standard is that every team should find ways to reduce time, improve quality, or both.
Design Phase One: Specification of Work Processes	How can people do it? What processes can people use to produce the products? How will we guide practice?	We'll use a systematic problem solving process the VP developed. There are worksheets and check-points to have the team's work approved by the CEO.
Design Phase Two: Specification of Instructional Processes	How does the overall design link learners and workplace? How does each unit?	People will be working on real workplace problems that mean something to them and the CEO.
Implementation and Evaluation	Are analysis and design done properly? Do the design and implementation reflect principles of adult learning and performance? Do they actually work?	We'll evaluate every project to assure that it follows the problem-solving steps. The steps will include specification and measure-ment of desired results.

group member is asked to write down at least one reason better teamwork would benefit him or her and at least one reason better teamwork would benefit the company. These items are compiled into one list.

Guided Practice

The trainer asks participants to identify a current production problem that re-quires good teamwork to solve and that would require even better teamwork to prevent. Participants generate three to five possible problems and select one they believe would be worthwhile and that could be solved during the next few weeks.

The trainer asks participants to identify several tasks to be done in order to verify that the problem exists and to obtain information about possible solutions. Each participant accepts responsibility for completing one or more of the tasks, one of which is to plan the next meeting. The trainer works with the volunteer to plan and run the next meeting.

The plan for the next meeting includes making a meeting agenda and assigning specific roles, e.g., a recorder to take minutes, someone to capture ideas on a flip chart, someone to facilitate, and two people to be followers who offer new ideas on any issue the leader raises. The trainer meets with each participant before the meeting to coach them on the specific roles. The meeting agenda calls for reviewing data verifying the problem, checking to see if all assigned tasks are complete, generating possible solutions to the problem, selecting a part of a solution to implement, and assigning tasks. The meeting ends with a new person accepting the role of leader and others accepting specific roles for the next meeting.

Demonstration of Mastery

Partial demonstrations of mastery occur during the meetings as people become more at ease and competent in taking on the various team roles. Other demonstrations of mastery occur as people complete assigned tasks, both between and within meetings. An overall demonstration of mastery occurs when team members report that the problem has been solved.

Real mastery of teamwork skills, however, cannot be demonstrated from one cooperative effort. Such mastery occurs over several months as several different teams are formed to solve specific problems. During that time, most people in the production unit serve on at least one problem-solving team and are involved in the teamwork required in the production area to implement the solutions generated by the several teams.

Analysis of Example

1. When did guided observation occur?
The guided observation occurred as people recalled past problems and successes and discussed what they had observed earlier. In a larger company (and in this company at a later time) people could have observed successfully functioning and poorly functioning teams by watching them in action.

The important thing is that guided observations must be of real events. The observation can occur both during and prior to the performance-based training sessions; if the observation itself is not guided, the guidance can occur as people rethink the historical events. Even if participants observe during a training session, the key learning occurs as they reflect on the observations and, with guidance, extract lessons that are meaningful in terms of future actions.

2. Why were problem-solving activities used?

Problem-solving activities are the most practical and beneficial vehicle for developing teamwork. Using problem solving as the vehicle yields multiple benefits: improved teamwork, improved teamwork skills, improved problem-solving skills, and problem solutions. The approach is practical because problem solving is a break from routine pressures and opens people's minds to new ways of doing things. It blends into the workplace readily and, at the same time, allows people to experience very specific successes that add value to the workplace.

3. Why weren't there any learning exercises in teamwork?

There were. The trainer coached between meetings and during meetings. Additional exercises were not needed because most people, at one time or another, have worked effectively in teams and, at one time or another, have worked ineffectively in teams. Ineffective teams have been so common in our school or work culture that people typically wait to determine whether to use teamwork skills. When people do not participate, others attempt to take control, and teamwork fails. In the example, coaching prevented that from happening.

It is not that individuals lack the skills of teamwork, but individuals have to *use* the skills fluently and in a real situation. The trainer in the example structured the meetings so that the skills were used as needed. It would have been possible, and possibly worthwhile, to have used any one of several standard team-building exercises to define roles or identify task and maintenance functions. In this case the trainer was available to facilitate teams as they did real work over the course of several months.

4. Why were roles assigned and rotated?

Roles were assigned to assure that all the necessary team functions would be performed. Assigning some of the work to each team member meant that everything got done and no one needed to do anything heroic to get it all to happen. The roles were rotated to give everyone practice in all roles, thereby assuring that each team member learned a full array of teamwork skills. The trainer coached individuals at every opportunity during routine interactions.

5. Why were some people called followers?

Good followers are a key element in leadership. Groups in which everyone tries to lead or push his or her own agenda are dysfunctional. Having someone designated as a follower eliminates many of the unproductive dynamics that can occur. The follower keeps things moving.

Because people exchange roles, leaders learn how important followers are and followers learn the importance of good leadership. When the teams are really functioning as teams, the roles blur. Each team member has the skills necessary to step into any role as needed. When this happens frequently and fluidly, it is a sign that a group has matured into a productive work team.

6. How did other production workers support the team?

As the problem-solving team implemented ideas, members made very specific requests, assigning specific tasks that yielded the overall results. When tasks were completed, results were obtained by teamwork and cooperation with others. This spread teamwork through the workplace naturally without establishing the team as an entity apart from the rest of the workers.

7. When should performance-based team building be used?

Any time team building is connected to a specific organizational goal, strategic initiative, or business issue, i.e., whenever performance improvement is sought.

8. How is effectiveness measured?

Effectiveness is determined by measuring the results achieved by the team and by the participation of each team member. These are the measurement questions:

- *Results*: Did the team achieve its goal, i.e., to improve output, decrease cycle time, improve quality, or reduce cost?
- *Participation*: Did each team member offer ideas and build on others' ideas by making constructive comments, volunteering for, and completing specific tasks during and between meetings?

How Performance-Based Team Building Works

Guided Observation

The discussion of problems that had occurred focused attention on workplace performance. By identifying which of the problems could be solved or prevented by better teamwork, participants learned that teamwork is not the solution to all problems, that it is part of the solution to some problems, and that they could identify when improved teamwork would and would not be beneficial. They also learned that teamwork, in their company, was intended to be win-win-win: team members, the company, and the customers all would win.

As the problem-solving/teamwork training sessions moved forward, each team member had multiple opportunities to see specific teamwork tasks performed well (and, occasionally, not so well). The trainer coached people in their roles and also called their attention to instances in which the tasks involved in the role had been performed well. Through observing many examples, participants could see that a particular style was not important, but that doing the tasks effectively was important to the team and to the problem-solving project.

Guided Practice

Team members practiced task functions and team functions. Task functions—doing their parts during a session and completing their assigned tasks between sessions—were the main focus. Team functions—leadership, followership, recording, facilitating—were practiced matter-of-factly as each participant learned new roles.

The purpose of the practice was always clear: doing what was necessary to solve the problem. Each task, whether performed by an individual or by the group, resulted in a product of some sort. Group products included written problem definitions and lists of alternative solutions, of obstacles (with tactics for overcoming each), of tasks to be completed before the next meeting, and of criteria for success. Real work and practice were blended so that much of the trainer's coaching was almost unnoticed by the participants.

The trainer evaluated performance quality throughout, only sharing with group members as needed. For example, the trainer asked each person to evaluate his or her own performance in a role or others' performance in a role he or she was to perform next. The trainer used the data for coaching individuals, but rarely presented it to the team as a whole. It was used either during a celebration of success or at a time when the group was "stuck" and needed the data to start moving again.

Demonstration of Mastery

The trainer had to be very attentive to mastery throughout the process. However, formal demonstrations of mastery occurred only at specific points when the group made a presentation to the CEO or to a work group. For example, when an alternative solution was selected and an implementation plan was developed, the group presented cost and benefit estimates for review, and when there were sufficient data to show that workplace performance was improving, celebrations were held. Over time, the presentations and celebrations became the major indicators of mastery. In addition, "mature" teams look, feel, and act like leaderless groups most of the time. Members move freely from one role to another as needed and only fall back on assigned roles when they are really stuck.

Tips and Caveats

1. The team-building process described is a simple one; however, it takes considerable skill by the trainer to make it both simple and effective. Most trainers acquire the skill through unplanned OJT. Consequently, a trainer new to the process should begin with a simple team problem within a work group made up of people who already tend to cooperate well with one another. It would be foolish for a novice trainer to begin with a major cross-functional problem involving people who have a long history of dysfunctional relationships.

2. It is easy for the trainer to believe that he or she can keep all the information in his or her head rather than collecting data on how well roles are performed by each person, what tasks are assigned and completed by whom between sessions, and what coaching suggestions have been made to the team and individuals. As a project moves forward, sloppy data keeping for team building has the same effect as sloppy data keeping for total quality management.

3. It is easy to focus too much on group maintenance functions. Many people who have not worked in a team environment are so accustomed to focusing on task functions that they view maintenance functions as a distraction or just plain silly. The guideline for the trainer, simple to state and difficult to follow, is: focus on group maintenance functions only when doing so will have a clear and immediate impact on a task problem.

4. It is difficult to do something well when you do not know what the goal is. Yet teams are often given poorly defined goals or objectives or problems or tasks or charges. Good teamwork skills must include refining, verifying, and clarifying the results that are to be achieved. For example, a team might be charged with coming up with plans for improving employee morale or improving a work process. Until there is a specific focus, the team will flounder.

5. It is difficult to do something well when you do not know what you are supposed to do. For example, exhorting people to "Participate!" will be less effective than asking for specifics, e.g., "When we brainstorm, each person is to contribute at least three ideas!" or "Who will contact the customer to find out how much they are likely to order this quarter?"

6. Participation is both offering and building. *Offering* involves making suggestions, volunteering for assignments, asking questions, etc. *Building* involves active

listening, using others' ideas constructively, etc. Offering to others and building on what others have offered generates healthy interactions in the group. Groups flounder when offering becomes demanding or dominating, when offering does not occur, and when people pursue their separate agendas rather than building on others'.

Becoming good at design, implementation, and maintenance of performance-based team building requires practice. Much of the practice can occur on the job. Some suggested practice exercises are included below.

Practice Exercises

The work of effective teams is so fluid that identifying just how they work has baffled researchers for years; so many things go wrong in ineffective teams that it is difficult to know what to focus on. We have, therefore, taken a simplified approach to improving teamwork, a performance-based approach that focuses not only on the fluid *activities* of team members but also on the *products* the team produces. The first guided observation exercise focuses on the *products* that team members produce during a problem-solving cycle. The second focuses on the *activities*.

Guided Observation Exercise One

This exercise is designed to identify products a team generates while solving a problem and to develop a tracking sheet to monitor team performance.

1. Either in one-on-one interviews or in a small group, ask people to tell stories about effective problem-solving efforts they have been part of. At another time or in another part of the interview, ask people to recall ineffective problem-solving efforts they have been part of.
2. Make a list of three to five key points at which a problem-solving effort can go wrong.
3. List key group products that, if prepared and reviewed, would prevent the problem-solving process from failing, e.g., a problem verification sheet or a project goal sheet. (Review Figure 3.1 for other ideas.)
4. Prepare a problem-solving tracking sheet, similar to the one in Figure 3.2, but using language appropriate to your workplace. The tracking sheet shows the products of each phase of a performance-based problem-solving process.

🗄 FIGURE 3.2. TEAM PROCESS AND PRODUCTS.

Phase	Products: Written Reports That Answer These Questions:	Start Time	End Time
Problem Definition	What is the problem?		
	What are possible causes?		
	What's working now?		
	What is our goal?		
Problem Solution	What are several possible solutions?		
	What solutions are recommended?		
	Why?		
Solution Implementation	What action steps will be taken when, by whom, where, how, and why?		
	What are the major obstacles?		
	How will each be overcome?		
	How will we measure success?		
Solution Evaluation	Who will collect what data, when, where, and how?		
	How will we assure the data are reliable?		
	Who will review the data?		
	How will we celebrate progress and success?		

Guided Observation Exercise Two

1. Either in one-on-one interviews or in a small, perhaps informally convened group, ask people to tell stories about effective teams they have been part of.
2. At another time or in another part of the interview ask people to tell stories about ineffective teams they have been part of.
3. Make a list of three to five characteristics of effective teams and three to five characteristics of ineffective teams. Do that by yourself or with the people from whom you collected the stories.
4. Edit the list down to three to seven items, in the language of your workplace, that describe characteristics of effective and ineffective teams.

Guided Observation Exercise Three

1. Observe a staff meeting, a project team meeting, or any other meeting in which people are supposedly working together to achieve a common goal.
2. Prepare (before the first observation or after it) an observation checklist based on a few of the items from Figure 3.3.
3. Based on the observation, identify one to three key skills that would improve the functioning of the team, if used more often.
4. Identify one to three things people do during or between meetings that interfere with teamwork.
5. Make a list of the key products (from Figure 3.1) that, if produced more explicitly, might improve the performance of the group.

Guided Practice Exercise One

1. Select a specific skill that you use more frequently when you are in meetings. (Consider using a skill from Figure 3.3 or from a tailored checklist.)
2. Identify opportunities for using the skill. Make a plan, perhaps including a list of situations in which you will use the skill, a sample script for how you will use it, or a checklist for monitoring when, where, and how to use it.
3. Practice using the skill, either in meetings on in one-on-one interactions.
4. After each practice episode, ask yourself and others, if appropriate:
   • What did I accomplish, using the skill?
   • What worked well?
   • How can I do better next time?

Guided Practice Exercise Two

1. Find an opportunity to facilitate teamwork skills.
2. Work with individuals to identify teamwork skills that they can practice during team meetings.
3. Meet with them regularly to coach and monitor their progress.
4. After each practice episode ask these questions:
   • What did we accomplish?
   • What skills did we use?
   • What worked well?
   • How can we do better next time?

Guided Practice Exercise Three

1. Find an opportunity to facilitate a team. Take the people on the team through Guided Practice Exercise One above.

FIGURE 3.3. ROLES, RESPONSIBILITIES, AND CRITICAL SKILLS FOR SUCCESSFUL PERFORMANCE IN GROUPS.

	For Leader	For Facilitator	For Recorder	For Followers
Major Role	Manage Work	Model Participation	Check Agreement	Participate
Major Responsibility	Meet or exceed standards	Satisfy more than frustrate individuals; become better at working together	Produce the product	Contribute to product; Achieve own goals
Key Skills (Offer and Build)	Ask leading questions about task: e.g., "I think we must produce this . . . . Do you all agree?"	Ask leading questions about participation: e.g., "I think we need to get everyone's ideas: X, what do you think?"	Ask leading questions about completion: e.g., "Here's what I have. Is that what we've agreed on?	"Offer ideas about content: e.g., "I think we could do it if . . ." "I'm not sure whether X's idea is different from Y's."

Role Summary: The leader focuses on the work process; the facilitator focuses on the people; the recorder focuses on the group product; the followers focus on the task at hand.

Responsibilities Summary: The *leader* is responsible for assuring that the work is done so that it meets organizational standards. The *facilitator* is responsible for assuring continuous improvement in meeting the needs of the people and the organization. The *recorder* is responsible for assuring that the product meets the group's standards. *Followers* are responsible for contributing to the product and achieving their own goals.

Key Skills of Group Members: Offering ideas and building on others' ideas by asking leading questions and by answering questions as well as possible.

2. Using a simplified version of Figure 3.2, discuss the problem-solving process and products. Prepare a description of the problem-solving process the group chooses to use. Assign roles for the next meeting, based on the roles defined in Figure 3.3.

3. Work with individuals to prepare them for their roles. Pay special attention to the specific products that the recorder (or recorders) will produce. Be sure that the leader knows which products are to be worked on at each point. Monitor during meetings and coach between meetings.

4. After each meeting and during between-meeting coaching sessions, ask these questions:
   - What did we accomplish?
   - What worked well?
   - What worked less well?
   - How can we do better next time?

Demonstration of Mastery

Several sets of skills must be mastered to become expert in analyzing situations and designing, implementing, and evaluating performance-based teamwork training in a problem-solving context. A form similar to Figure 3.4 can be used to monitor progress. The form provides a place to track the guided observation and practice exercises as well as additional projects. Each practice project will yield products that can be used to assess progress.

FIGURE 3.4. DEMONSTRATIONS OF MASTERY.

Project	Goal	Start	End	Comments/Results

CHAPTER FOUR

PERFORMANCE-BASED DEVELOPMENT

An Overview

Where Are We Going?

This chapter focuses on helping individuals create and implement developmental plans, tools for guiding people as they do projects. Developmental plans add value in two ways: (1) they solve problems or help an employer or a client organization innovate and (2) they enable individuals to acquire valuable knowledge, skills, and attitudes.

- *Purpose*: To implement problem solving and innovation projects that improve current performance and develop people for the future.
- *Benefits*: Modern organizations must develop internally and rapidly to keep pace with a rapidly changing external environment. Internal development that solves current problems and helps the company position for the future assures survival and long-term prosperity.
- *Drawbacks*: Investing in development for the future can put a strain on people's current energy and on an organization's cash flow; failing to develop jeopardizes future prospects. Striking a balance between current and future issues is difficult.

How Shall We Get There?

First, we will consider an example to see how guided observation, guided practice, and demonstration of mastery can be used in performance-based development.

Then we will analyze the example to see how it relates to the specific setting and begin to understand how it could be used in other settings.

Finally, we will look at performance-based development to see how it can be used as a vehicle for continuous improvement, individual development, and organization development. For example, a manager can establish developmental plans with people in a work group, encouraging them to learn new technologies. Using the new learnings to solve current work problems makes the development performance-based; selecting new learnings for the future makes the learning developmental. It might work like this:

- *Guided Observation*: People are encouraged to identify ideas for improving how things are done, about emerging technologies, and about marketplace trends. Individual and work-group plans are devised. Each individual drafts a developmental plan; the unit manager, group leader, or group as a whole drafts a developmental plan for the unit and a plan for coordinating and approving implementation of plans.
- *Guided Practice*: Approved plans are implemented. Each includes vehicles for new learning and specific action plans to solve current performance problems or making specific workplace innovations. Typically, a plan includes progress checks and mentoring or coaching.
- *Demonstration of Mastery*: Mastery of the new learning is demonstrated through the implementation of performance-improvement projects.

Some tips and caveats are given, as well as a selection of practice exercises for using performance-based development to develop ourselves and others.

How Will We Know We've Arrived?

The following self-assessment checklist can be used:

Self-Assessment Checklist
Can I describe:

- At least one new thing that I could learn that would help me do my current work more competently and that would be useful to me in a few years?

- Two or three advantages to individuals and to an employer of having developmental plans that focus on improving current performance *and* positioning for future challenges?
- Two or three disadvantages of developmental plans that focus on future challenges but do not bring improvements in current performance?
- Similarities between designing and implementing developmental plans and on-the-job training?
- Ways to use the developmental planning process to prepare myself for a promotion or a different job?
- How a manager could use completed developmental plans to support recommending someone for promotion?
- How developmental plans could assure the success of newly established problem-solving teams?
- How developmental plans could support the implementation of a strategic plan for an organization or a department?
- Two or three similarities between the purposes of strategic plans for organizations and developmental plans for individuals?
- How developmental plans could be used as part of career development or management development or supervisory training?

Doing some of the practice exercises at the end of the chapter will help identify other opportunities for using developmental plans. Each practice exercise is another step along the never-ending journey of self-development. Be sure to put doing projects that enable you to improve at the developmental process on your personal developmental plan!

A tracking form is included to measure your progress and mastery.

Performance-Based Example

The manager of an HRD unit in a large company (seven thousand employees, $3 billion in sales) believed that professionals must continue to learn or become progressively less competent. Managing an HRD group that modeled creeping incompetence seemed doubly self-defeating. The company leaders were satisfied with the success of the company. It was cash rich and growing rapidly. The HRD manager decided to initiate a developmental program for HRD staff members, a simple process that could be used by any manager, improve current performance, and develop staff members.

Guided Observation

Staff members were encouraged to identify areas in which some aspect of the unit's work performance could be improved. Brainstorming sessions were held during staff meetings. When ideas were generated that the group or an individual deemed valuable, a project was undertaken. For example, managing the organization's educational assistance program required careful and time-consuming logistical work. It also involved policy formulation and approval by the manager each time new needs were brought up. A project was undertaken to develop a computerized system for tracking and approving requests for educational assistance. The necessary data was collected to identify and support policy formulation and administration.

Guided Practice

The person in charge of the educational assistance program drafted a developmental plan that included learning how to select or design a computerized system. The manager's development plan included learning more about policy formulation through reading and dealing with two specific policy issues.

Demonstration of Mastery

Mastery was demonstrated when the computerized system was in operation. The new system reduced the amount of time required to process educational assistance applications, reduced errors, and improved customer satisfaction. Mastery was also demonstrated when policies formulated were approved and accepted by users and beneficiaries of the educational assistance program.

Analysis of Example

1. Is that all?
Developmental plans involving problem solving and innovation were established and implemented by all members of the HRD staff. Each plan was simple, aimed at a specific improvement in current performance, and involved learning what the staff member and manager believed would be beneficial to the individual.

2. How did the developmental plans relate to the routine HRD work?
The plans involved solving current problems or implementing the department's strategic plan, so they were closely related. In addition, the manager required documented growth for performance reviews, promotions, and salary adjustments.

People were expected to devote a few hours each week to personal development and strategic development.

3. How did people respond to the developmental plans?

Everyone agreed with the concept; however, there were individual differences in how much time and energy were spent and in the results achieved. Some people developed quickly, others dragged their feet.

4. Why did people respond differently?

Development, by definition, means growing from where you are. Staff members were in different places in their personal development as well as in their professional development. One staff member who was a new parent did little with the developmental plan during the few months after the baby was born. Staff members who were actively involved in school or church did less on theirs when the school or church activities were especially heavy. Newer staff members tended to have more to learn so their developmental plans contained relatively specific and easier improvements. More experienced staff members' plans were more complex. For example, they learned to improve relationships with specific HRD clients or learned to work in teams on complex cross-functional projects.

5. Can the process be used outside of HRD?

The needs for development are enormous in many areas of an organization. Some managers, such as the HRD manager mentioned here, understand the need for development and welcome specific, practical, and effective procedures that support development. Other managers, including HRD managers, either do not understand the need or do not know how to proceed.

On the other hand, some managers are not interested in developing employees for various reasons. They may want to hold costs down and believe that if people improve they will want more pay; they may think that if they develop people, they will lose them; they may believe that if they develop people, the people will compete with them for scarce rewards. These fears can be realistic.

6. How much management time does it take?

One answer is about thirty minutes per person per week. At the other extreme is just enough time to do a perfunctory performance appraisal once a year. The real answer is that the amount of time per person varies according to the situation, the employee, and the manager. One way to estimate the time needed by a specific manager is to find out how much time that manager spends in staff meetings or in individual conversations with direct reports. That same time can be used productively to support developmental plans.

7. How can a manager develop employees and do anything else?

One manager's approach is to organize the work to assure that development occurs. Assign work responsibilities to teams rather than individuals. Here is how one manager solved the problem:

1. The manager announced that each employee was to remain accountable for the same things; however, each person was to identify at least one process-improvement, quality-improvement, or cost-reduction project.
2. The proposed projects were reviewed at a staff meeting. Teams were formed to work on them.
3. Each staff member was asked to lead one improvement project outside of his or her own area. Some teams were made up of two people.
4. The team leader was accountable for assuring that the improvement project was successful and for reporting progress to the manager.

The manager's rationale was that the procedure would assure crosstraining, develop technical skills, develop project-management skills, and develop employee ability to work across functions.

8. How much value is added?

Each manager can estimate the value by noticing the impact on morale and on how staff spend discretionary time, by tracking implementation of a strategic plan, by tracking the new or improved services offered by the unit, and by tracking the cumulative value added from the problem-solving and innovation projects completed. The value of a well-managed performance-based development process can add up significantly over time.

How Performance-Based Development Works

The manager who supports performance-based development can use it as a tool for organization development, individual development, and continuous improvement.

Guided Observation

Asking people to identify opportunities for improvement and then take action sets a constructive tone for the workplace. It is very important that the development be linked to the work of the unit:

- Development, if linked, is real, rather than pie in the sky, a promise kept rather than a promise made.
- The development pays off for the people involved, including the manager who supports it; it also pays off to the organization in the future.
- One future need is to find people to commit to continuous improvement.

Guided Practice

It is important to give people guidance on their efforts to develop. A developmental plan typically gives a variety of sources such as:

- Reading manuals, articles, or books
- Attending seminars, workshops, or university classes
- Observing people who are doing something similar
- Working on a team with people who already know how to do something
- Having regular meetings with the manager or another mentor

The major source for guidance, however, comes from actually doing the performance-improvement projects themselves.

Demonstration of Mastery

An important feature of performance-based development is that every developmental activity (or set of activities) yields a specific and tangible product or result. These add current value that can be evaluated. In addition, contribution to future performance can be estimated and sometimes measured. For example, the project presented in the example contributed to the efficiency and effectiveness of the HRD program. The specific skills learned by the person in charge have a lasting value for that person if he or she continues to develop administrative systems, management systems, or computer utilization systems. The motivational effect on the person being developed can also be seen by the person's eagerness to make future improvements.

Tips and Caveats

1. People will, and should, develop at different rates, depending on situational factors as well as their own characteristics.
2. Development tends to occur in spurts. It is easy to believe that a person who just happens to be in a growth spurt has a much greater potential for the fu-

ture than someone who happens to be in a slow-growth or steady state. Remember that today's tortoise could become tomorrow's hare and vice versa.

3. Providing equal opportunity also means giving everyone equal opportunities to develop. Managers who focus only on a few people are running unnecessary risks of lowering morale and encouraging litigation.

4. Part of a manager's responsibility is to wisely manage all the resources provided by the organization. Managers who are not developing human resources are not fulfilling their responsibilities. The challenges facing current managers make it a very dangerous to ignore that responsibility.

Practice Exercises

Learning to facilitate individual development is a very valuable skill set that can be applied not only to helping others develop but to helping develop your own potential. Of course, acquiring and improving this skill set takes practice that should continue throughout your professional life.

Guided Observation Exercise One

1. Interview several people within one organization. Include someone you believe is an excellent developer of people, someone you believe is not or is typical of most managers, and a person whom you believe to be developing rapidly. Ask them questions such as these:

   - What experiences have you had that have supported or stimulated your development?
   - Why is modeling professional development a good way for managers to encourage people to develop?
   - Why is it primarily your own responsibility to initiate your own professional development?
   - Why is supporting employee development an important management responsibility?
   - What are some things managers do every day that interfere with the development of others?
   - What are some routine things that managers can do to support employee development?
   - Why does encouraging people to work together to solve problems support their development?
   - What are some easy and effective ways to develop people?

2. Follow up, if you wish, with in-depth interviews to discover either exemplary practices or obstacles.

3. Compile the reasons given for supporting development and their ideas on how to do it. Compare what you have compiled with the ideas about performance-based development presented above. To what extent do they support, supplement, complement, or contradict one another?

Guided Observation Exercise Two

1. Search for your own developmental opportunities related to areas in which you would like to perform well in the future. Ask yourself questions similar to these:
   - What are some recurring problems or situations that I encounter frequently that consume a lot of time and are necessary to deal with?
   - Which of the problems/situations might I prevent or handle more easily if I did something differently?
   - What could I do or learn that would help me deal with them?
   - What are some changes that are occurring that will influence what I do in the future?
   - What can I do that would help me now and prepare me to deal with those changes?

2. After thinking about and working with these questions for awhile, identify three or four projects that would enable you to learn something that would help and that could be completed in a few days, weeks, or months.

3. Think about the value, to you and to your workplace, of doing one or more of the projects:
   - What would be better if you did the project(s)?
   - What would be worse?
   - What would stay the same if you do not do the project(s)?

Guided Practice Exercise One

1. Select one of the developmental projects that you have identified, one you believe will add significant value and that can be completed within a few weeks.

2. Construct a plan for doing the project. If you are skilled at project management, use those skills; if you are not or if you would prefer, use the worksheet in Figure 4.1 as inspiration for designing one that works better for you.

3. Implement the project plan.

4. Monitor the project as you do it and review results when it is completed:
   - What worked well?

- What did not work as well?
- How can you do the next project better?
- What were the major results?

Guided Practice Exercise Two

1. Find a client who would like to develop and who might benefit from guidance and support.
2. Interview the client, asking questions similar to those in Guided Observation Exercise Two.

FIGURE 4.1. DEVELOPMENTAL PROJECT PLANNING WORKSHEET.

Goals/Purposes	
What current performance do you seek to improve? What is the activity, and what results or products does the activity produce?	
What are the long-term benefits to you? to others? How can developing in this area help you perform better in the future?	
Implementation Plan	
Guided Observation: What information will you collect to verify the value of the improvement? of the new learning?	
Guided Practice: What will be the sequence of tasks or subprojects you complete?	
Demonstration of Mastery: What are the benchmarks and progress checks along the way?	
What measures of timeliness, quality, or cost will you use to tell you that the project was successful?	

3. Show the client the project that you completed in Guided Practice Exercise One. Offer to help the client plan and implement a developmental project.
4. If the client agrees, do it; if the client does not agree, approach others until you find someone who is ready to put in the effort involved.
5. Work with the client to evaluate the project, asking these and other questions:
   • What worked well?
   • What did not work well?
   • How can we do better next time?
   • What were the major results?

Guided Practice Exercise Three

1. Find as a client a manager who believes in developing people. Offer to help the manager implement developmental projects with his or her staff.
2. Show the manager some of the work you completed in Guided Practice Exercises One and Two. Ask the manager to work with you to modify or refine the approach so it will fit the setting.
3. Use this modified approach to do a project for the manager's development.
4. Fine tune the approach.
5. Devise a plan, with the manager, for supporting individual development of others.
6. Implement the plan and evaluate the process and results.

Guided Practice Exercise Four

1. Repeat the process with another manager.
2. Repeat the process with a group of managers as part of a performance-based workshop in development of people.

Demonstration of Mastery Exercises

One of the key features of performance-based development is that each developmental activity involves learning and application. Application is a demonstration of mastery. As you practice over several applications, you develop from novice to expert. It is a matter of doing the projects, finding out what works and what does not, and incorporating as much of what works as possible in future projects.

The Demonstrations of Mastery table in Figure 4.2 can be used to track progress toward mastery of any skill set involved. Figure 4.3, Toward Mastery of Performance-Based Instruction Skills, can be used to monitor completion of at least one project for each step in performance-based instruction. Record projects you completed in Chapters Two and Three now.

FIGURE 4.2. DEMONSTRATIONS OF MASTERY.

Project	Goal	Start	End	Comments/Results
Guided Observation 1	Identify value and obstacles			
Guided Observation 2	Identify personal development opportunities			
Guided Practice 1	Implement a development plan			
Guided Practice 2	Facilitate development plan implementation			
Guided Practice 3	Help a manager establish development plans			
Guided Practice 4	Help groups of managers establish development plans			

FIGURE 4.3. TOWARD MASTERY OF PERFORMANCE-BASED INSTRUCTION SKILLS.

Project	Goal	Start	End	Comments/Results
Chapter 2 (Performance-Based OJT)				
Chapter 3 (Performance-Based Teamwork)				
Chapter 4 (Professional Development)				
Chapter 5 (Job Feedback Design)				
Chapter 6 (Using Job Aids)				
Chapter 7 (The PBI Paradigm)				
Chapter 8 (Conversion to PBI)				
Chapter 9 (Transfer of Training)				
Chapter 10 (Needs Assessment)				
Chapter 11 (Structured Design of PBI)				
Chapter 12 (Integrating Evaluation)				
Chapter 13 (Learning to Learn)				

CHAPTER FIVE

PERFORMANCE-BASED INSTRUCTION AND THE HAWTHORNE EFFECT

An Overview

Where Are We Going?

This chapter features one of the most powerful and cost-effective instructional designs. Because it occurs on the job, it is called the job-feedback design.

- *Purpose*: The job-feedback design has three main purposes. It can:
  — supplement other training designs to assure that training has an impact on on-the-job performance
  — reduce the amount of costly off-the-job training
  — support continuous improvement in performance
- *Benefits*: The design has a very high benefit to cost ratio. Once installed, it becomes an ongoing training and performance support system for continuous improvement.
- *Drawbacks*: The design is powerful because so many jobs lack adequate feedback; however, that is a two-edged sword. Feedback may be inadequate for any number of reasons, e.g., the purposes of the job are not clear, there are no performance standards, people prefer the challenges of confusion over the challenges of competence, people resist attempts to measure their performance systematically, or people believe that their jobs change too rapidly to measure systematically. All these problems and more must be overcome to use

the job-feedback design. In addition the design does not look like what people expect when they request training. A manager who requests a training course might conclude that the HRD professional is being unresponsive to the request and meddling in the manager's job. In some work environments the problems simply cannot be overcome.

How Shall We Get There?

First, we will consider the most famous example of the job-feedback design, the events that occurred at the Western Electric Hawthorne plant. Then we will analyze the example to learn new lessons from it. We will see that the key elements of performance-based instruction were accidentally put in place. We will look at the key elements more closely to see how they could be applied in other settings. Next, we will consider some tips and caveats and, last, select from an array of practice exercises.

How Will We Know We've Arrived?

First, a self-assessment checklist can be used to assess understanding:

> ### *Self-Assessment Checklist*
> Do I know:
>
> - How the design can be used to improve performance on the job?
> - How the design can be used to support other training designs to assure transfer to the workplace?
> - How to use the design as a way to identify specific gaps in knowledge?
> - How to use the design to respond quickly to a training request and still have the time necessary to develop excellent training?
> - How to use the design to evaluate use and impact of what has been learned in a performance-based training program?
> - The key elements of the design?
> - How the key elements of the design exemplify performance-based instruction?
> - What to say if someone wants to know whether this means that the usual interpretations of the Hawthorne effect are wrong?
> - How to learn more about the job-feedback design for professional development?

The guided practice exercises at the end of the chapter can be used to discover specific opportunities to use the design. We can design and do several additional projects in which we practice the skills involved in implementing the job-feedback design and determine how well we have mastered them. We can, in the process, measure the value added.

A Job-Feedback Design Example

The Hawthorne effect is probably the most famous example of performance-based instruction. As the story is usually told, engineers at the Western Electric Hawthorne plant, in Cicero, Illinois, set out to do an experiment on the effects of lighting on workplace performance. They improved the lighting and performance improved. They improved the lighting again and performance improved more. After seeing improvements a few times, they returned the lighting to its original condition, expecting to see performance fall back to earlier levels. To their surprise, performance improved again!

The usual interpretation is that paying attention to workers improves performance, independent of anything else. Social scientists use the term "Hawthorne effect" to describe improvements brought about by paying attention to people. The implication is that it is a good idea to pay attention to people. But as every manager already knows, just paying attention to people is not enough. If we look at the Hawthorne story in more detail, we will see that there are a few very specific ways of paying attention that result in improved performance and many ways of paying attention that just do not work.

- *Guided Observation*: When the engineers began the experiment, they were concerned about the workers and wanted to be fair. Not knowing how the experiment would turn out, the engineers did not know how the people should be paid for their work; pay had been based on a work-measurement system, but the engineers feared that the work measurement standards in effect might not be appropriate during the experiment. They decided that, if performance improved as they expected, it would only be fair to pay people more, so they initiated a piece-work system. The engineers' decision provided an important element of the job-feedback design. Knowing that they were paid by the item, people had a clear goal: produce more good items. They kept track of how many items were produced.
- *Guided Practice*: Knowing how they were doing minute by minute set the stage for guided practice. The workers could try different tactics and see which tactics resulted in better performance. If a worker thought of a better way of doing

the work, he or she asked the engineers to make changes in the way the work was set up; when the engineers followed the suggestions, it was possible to reach higher levels of performance.

- *Demonstration of Mastery*: Mastery was shown by the steady improvement in performance as the workers learned better ways of doing the job and as the engineers supported performance by taking suggestions seriously and making process improvements. The reason performance improved was that a goal-directed, incentive-based, feedback-guided, participative-management system was established. Performance improved each time the lighting was improved, not because of the lighting but because the management system lead to continuous learning and achievement of higher levels of mastery.

Analysis of the Example

1. How do we know that the effect was not a result of monetary incentives?

The gradual improvement and associated changes in work procedures shows that more was involved than a simple incentive change. The pay-for-performance system was important in supporting the other changes. For example, it is unlikely that as many suggestions would have been made without the monetary incentive; it is *extremely* unlikely that as many suggestions would have been made if the suggestions had been ignored. We know from other research that feedback systems can often improve performance without added incentives.

2. What lessons do the Hawthorne studies provide?

There are three specific lessons for human resource development professionals:

1. Use a powerful design that provides learners with clear goals, adequate incentives, opportunities for guided practice, and clear feedback on improvement!
2. Include the necessary conditions for transfer of training: clear goals, adequate incentives, opportunities for guided practice, and clear feedback on performance!
3. Include the necessary conditions for supporting performance on the job: clear goals, adequate incentives, adequate tools, opportunities for guided practice, and clear feedback on performance!

In short, the Hawthorne studies illustrate the Gilbert (1996) concept of the behavior engineering model and the Rummler and Brache (1995) concept of the performance system.

3. When should the job-feedback design be used?

Question 2 provides the answer. The job-feedback design can be used:

- As a form of on-the-job training; it has the necessary ingredients to support continuous improvement
- To support transfer of training; it can and probably should be used as an adjunct to any training design
- As a paradigm for managing performance

Is there any doubt that workers and organizations benefit from clear goals, adequate incentives, adequate tools, opportunities for guided practice, and clear feedback on performance?

4. Does everyone interpret the Hawthorne effect this way?

The most common interpretation is that new things, e.g., team building or process reengineering or performance-based instruction, are likely to be valued for a short time just because people are excited about the new thing and put their best effort into it. After the newness wears off and people have forgotten why they were excited about it, the effectiveness and value can diminish.

Managers and researchers know that it is just common sense that the act of measuring performance can have an effect on it. But the effect of being watched wears off quickly unless the other elements of the job-feedback design are also present. The notion that "paying attention to workers" is a good thing to do was and is correct, but we must pay attention to the right things.

5. Why is this interpretation of the Hawthorne effect better?

The interpretation, first published by Parsons (1974), is plausible because of a substantial body of research showing specific effects of each of the variables manipulated during the Hawthorne studies: goal setting, incentives, feedback, coaching, and guided practice (Kopelman, 1986). Doing them together, as was done at Hawthorne, can be quite powerful. Many additional studies have been done that show that "paying attention" in these specific ways supports improved performance.

How the Job-Feedback Design Works

Guided Observation

Feedback guides observation. For the Hawthorne studies, providing timely feedback about the number of units produced enabled the workers to see what worked effectively. In general, providing feedback on the timeliness, quality, and/or cost of performance products is necessary to support good performance.

The necessity of feedback might seem obvious, but it has gone largely unnoticed, possibly because supervisors are often used in place of direct feedback.

That is, the supervisor receives information about timeliness, quality, or cost of performance—though often not on a timely or systematic basis—and then tries to guide the workers. The supervisor functions as a link in a feedback system, but because the feedback typically is not clear, supervisors have been unable to provide good feedback.

Guided Practice

Information about performance makes guided practice possible, but efforts to improve must be allowed and supported. In the Hawthorne studies, the workers were able to improve performance on their own, but they also could make suggestions to the engineers which, when followed, made additional improvement possible. In general, having clear goals and feedback set the stage for guided practice; with careful coaching, a recognition that all attempts to improve will not be successful (i.e., learners/workers will make errors), and provision of adequate tools and materials, the practice can be successful.

Demonstration of Mastery

Excellence in performance is simply performance to a high standard or the best performance to date. In the job-feedback design, we seek to assure that performance reaches a high standard and that it continues to improve. We seek not only high standards of performance but also to make the best performance today into tomorrow's standard.

Typically, people using the job-feedback design will set a standard that is thought to be attainable by the learners/workers. As with a competently run management-by-objectives system, the learners/workers are involved in setting a standard that is both attainable and economically productive. The standard is adjusted upward from time to time as proficiency improves or as performance is reengineered.

Tips and Caveats

1. In the bad old days, when workers regularly achieved a high standard, management simply set the standard higher. The workers' reward for high performance was simply more work. This still occurs, but we know a much better way to do it: Share the benefits of the improved productivity with those who produce more. That is what Taylor recommended in his scientific management approach in the early 1900s, it is what occurred at the Hawthorne plant

a few decades later, and it was initiated at Lincoln Electric about fifty years ago. Sharing the rewards of productivity improvement works.

2. It is easy to draw false conclusions from the summaries of case studies in the management literature; worse, the false conclusions are likely to be satisfying enough to hide important lessons. We should guard against false conclusions by looking for alternative explanations.

3. Sometimes the truth is lost because it is obvious: it is obvious that people cannot perform intelligently, effectively, and consistently if they lack information about how well they are doing. This is obvious to each of us as we try to do our work; yet, lacking feedback ourselves, we neglect to provide others with as much feedback as we could give.

4. Giving feedback does not mean dumping on people nor praising them; it is providing information about performance relevant to goals that enables the person receiving it to maintain good performance, improve performance, and feel good about the results. Feedback requires us to give information about trends in performance.

5. Feedback is about performance, not about who did it; unfortunately, if someone consistently performs well (or poorly), we slip into the habit of saying the person is a good (or poor) performer. This bad habit creates even more problems.

6. Good feedback is valuable and rare. Performance deficiencies are often caused by feedback deficiencies. Wise instructional designers will attempt to use the job-feedback design often:
   - instead of other training
   - supplemented by coaching (on-the-job training)
   - before training (installing a job-feedback design right away to obtain immediate results)
   - after training as follow-up support and evaluation of the impact of training

Practice Exercises

Guided Observation Exercise One

1. To do a rough assessment of how much room there is for improvement in workplace feedback, select ten people who are currently employed, perhaps in one organization, more or less randomly. Interview each, asking questions such as:
   - What is the purpose of your work?
   - Do you have specific goals?

- How do you tell how well you are doing?
- If you do something very well, does anyone notice?
- If you do something very poorly, does anyone notice?
- If you had good feedback, could you accomplish more or better work?
- How easy is it to get ahead in your workplace without performing well?

2. When you finish, score the results according to how many people have good feedback about how well they are doing. In the authors' experience:
- 0–1 is common
- 2–3 is unusual
- 4 or more is rare

Guided Observation Exercise Two

1. Select one major task for a job you are familiar with and can observe. The task should be one of the most important ones the performer does. Try to select a task that produces a document or other permanent product, e.g., a customer interaction that results in an order, a production run that results in X widgets, a library search that results in X usable references, a problem-solving process that results in specific actions.
2. Use the Feedback Adequacy Checklist, Figure 5.1, to identify strengths and weaknesses in feedback to the performer. Using the checklist requires you to make judgments; if you have not received guided practice in working with feedback systems, just use common sense for now. The Bibliography and References section has several helpful readings on this topic for later use.
3. Count the number of specific feedback deficiencies you find. Repeat this exercise several times to determine the most common weaknesses in your environment.
4. If you have done the exercise as a serious needs assessment, do a Pareto chart of your results.

Guided Practice Exercise One

1. Based on your work in the Guided Observation exercises, make improvements in the feedback for one or more persons and one or more tasks. For example, performance data relevant to customer standards may be weak. Timeliness of response is usually very important to customers. Consider setting up a way to track how many times the task is completed on time, using number of times per hour or week or day, or whatever is appropriate.
2. Talk to the performer about what levels of performance he or she wants to achieve; if the performer sets improvement goals, cheer when progress is made and help the performer problem solve if not enough progress is made.

▣ FIGURE 5.1. FEEDBACK ADEQUACY CHECKLIST.

Performer:		Date:	Analyst:
Dimensions of Feedback		**Adequacy**	**Comments**
Are performance data readily available?	Relevant to the performer's standards?	Yes/No?	
	Relevant to customer standards?	Yes/No?	
Do the data relate clearly to goals?	Personal goals of the performer?	Yes/No?	
	Organizational goals?	Yes/No?	
Are all three parts of the feedback loop present?	1: Clear data?	Yes/No?	
	2: Relevant to goals and standards?	Yes/No?	
	3: Relevant to specific actions?	Yes/No?	
Are the data adequately displayed?	Focused on relevant dimensions?	Yes/No?	
	Timely to guide performance corrections?	Yes/No?	
	Timely to guide performance strategies?	Yes/No?	
	Displayed over time to show trends?	Yes/No?	
Are management responses to the data properly balanced?	Enough positive reactions to maintain or strengthen effort?	Yes/No?	
	Enough negative reactions to show need for specific corrections?	Yes/No?	
	More positive than negative to show support for performers?	Yes/No?	

3. Track the performance dimension for a time. Ask these questions frequently:
   - What is your goal?
   - What progress are you making?
   - What is working well?

- How can you improve?
- How can I help?

Guided Practice Exercise Two

1. Working with a friendly colleague, do Guided Practice Exercise One for some aspect of your own work. When approaching the colleague, ask for help.
2. Volunteer to help your colleague with a similar project.

Guided Practice Exercise Three

1. Engage a manager in conversation about feedback, perhaps beginning with questions similar to those in Guided Observation Exercise One above.
2. If the manager appears receptive, volunteer to use the Feedback Adequacy Checklist, Figure 5.1, to take a look at the feedback for the work unit or for the manager.
3. If the manager agrees, do the assessment.
4. Help the work group devise more effective feedback systems for their work. This will work especially well if you have worked with the group to build teamwork, as outlined in Chapter Three. In fact, improving feedback is an excellent problem-solving project for any work group.
5. Work with the group, supporting and coaching as they begin using the feedback system.
6. At frequent intervals, ask these questions:
   - How does having the feedback help?
   - What is working well?
   - What is not working well?
   - How can we improve?

Demonstration of Mastery Exercises

The skills involved in improving performance by improving feedback can be acquired by further on-the-job practice; the performance improvements pay for the effort involved.

If you choose to become expert with this skill set, you might use a chart such as Figure 5.2 to track your performance. The start/end data will help you determine whether your cycle time is improving, although there will be variability associated with the complexity of each project. If you graph the data, the trend lines will show whether or not you are improving. If you use the results to record estimates of the dollar value added by each project, you can also track the cumulative value added and monitor trends to show whether or not the value per project is increasing.

FIGURE 5.2. DEMONSTRATIONS OF MASTERY.

Project	Goal	Start	End	Results

CHAPTER SIX

PERFORMANCE-BASED INSTRUCTION AND JOB AIDS

An Overview

Where Are We Going?

The focus of this chapter is on job aids, what they are, why they are valuable instructional tools, and how to design and use a few simple and powerful job aids.

- *Purpose*: Job aids are used to reduce training costs, increase reliability in performing infrequent tasks, assure consistency of performance across multiple workers, and make changes in procedures easier to implement.
- *Benefits*: In addition to the benefits implied above, using them can improve the quality of training while decreasing lead time and cycle time for training design and implementation.
- *Drawbacks*: Although some job aids such as simple flow charts or checklists are easy to construct, some are quite complex and difficult, such as complex decision tables and electronic support systems. Job aids are tools and, as with any tool, can be used ineffectively; they must be properly designed, people must learn to use them, and people must actually use them.

How Shall We Get There?

We will consider an example to see how job aids can bring very complex and strategically important information to people, putting it at their fingertips, rather than in their heads. We will analyze the example to see how the job aid worked in the specific setting and begin to see how other job aids (e.g., a recipe, a math formula, a list of steps, a worksheet such as the IRS form 1040, a template for desktop publishing, or a template for using a software spreadsheet) can be useful. Then we will consider some tips and caveats before doing several practice exercises. The practice exercises introduce and provide examples of two specific types of job aids: Situation-Interpretation-Action Charts and Performance Episode Flow Charts.

How Will We Know We've Arrived?

We can easily understand what job aids are and why they are useful, but we must go further and actually use them. Attaining mastery takes considerable practice and study. Books by Rossett and Gautier-Downes (1992), Horn (1976, 1989), and Lineberry and Bullock (1980) are outstanding, as is a chapter by Nelson (1997).

Use the following checklist to illustrate your understanding of the basic concepts:

Self-Assessment Checklist
Do I know how job aids can be used:
- To guide observation of work quality, work procedures, and training exercises?
- To guide practice?
- To guide assessment of *mastery*?
- To communicate standards or mastery criteria for highly effective performance?
- As part of any performance-based instruction exercise, course, or program to provide information or procedures?
- To help people learn procedures quickly and to help them remember complex or infrequently used procedures?
- For just-in-time on-the-job training so that people do not have to wait for a training class?

Can I identify half a dozen specific situations in which using job aids would be beneficial?

Can I see how to reduce the cost and improve the effectiveness of at least one specific HRD program by using job aids?

A Job-Aid Example

A specialty manufacturing company receives several new work orders each month. If the engineer estimates manufacturing costs (time, materials, etc.) accurately, the company makes money. If the engineer underestimates the costs, either the company loses money or bills the customer for the higher cost (at the risk of alienating customers). If the engineer overestimates costs, the company is likely to lose the job to a competitor. In short, the engineer's ability to estimate costs accurately is critical to company success, but no one else knows how. The process the company took to develop a course of instruction for estimating is shown in Figure 6.1 and also described under the headings of guided observation, guided practice, and demonstration of mastery below.

Guided Observation

The trainer interviewed the engineer, observed him or her make estimates, and attempted to capture the procedure with a job aid in the form of an expert system program. After several tries, the job aid seemed to work, although not as well as the engineer. Three people who were to be trained to estimate observed the engineer in action and observed tests of various drafts of the job aid.

Guided Practice

After the job aid was finished, the three people were trained to use it. They knew the importance of accurate job estimates, as described above. The next step in the training procedure was to have the engineer interview the customer to obtain needed information. Then the trainee made an estimate using the job aid and compared it to the estimate made by the expert. After about five attempts, the trainee could make an estimate almost as quickly and accurately as the engineer.

The next step was to have the trainee interview the customer (with the customer's permission) while the engineer listened. If the trainee performed adequately, the trainee and the engineer estimated the job; if not, the engineer took over the interview. The trainees also quickly learned the interview process, because they had a job aid in the form of a list of the basic and follow-up interview questions.

Demonstration of Mastery

Guided practice continued until mastery was achieved. Mastery was defined as producing ten estimates in succession in which the actual cost of the job was within

FIGURE 6.1. PROBLEM/OPPORTUNITY ANALYSIS.

Project Phase	Key Questions	Sample Answers
Specification of Business Need	What is the strategic or current business need for performance improvement?	Everything is OK now, but if Anthony is run over by a bus, we're in deep trouble. Everyone else who has tried estimating hasn't been able to do it.
Specification of Performance Requirements	What performance products are needed? What standards? What performance support?	Quick, accurate estimates for an extremely wide variety of jobs. The only performance support is a spreadsheet he uses to do the actual calculations and generate the estimate.
Design Phase One: Specification of Work Processes	How can people do it? What processes can people use to produce the products? How will we guide practice?	We don't know how he does it. We'll have to do some careful "guided observation" of Anthony!
Design Phase Two: Specification of Instructional Processes	How does the overall design link learners and workplace? How does each unit?	We'll use guided practice with old jobs and then with some new and real ones, but only after we figure out what Anthony is doing.
Implementation and Evaluation	Are analysis and design done properly? Do the design and implementation reflect principles of adult learning and performance? Do they actually work?	We'll be able to tell by having a couple of trainees use whatever we come up with. We'll have them practice with the old orders until they can do them and then have them try some new ones with Anthony watching them like a hawk!

10 percent of the estimate, the job was completed on time, and the customer was satisfied.

Analysis of Example

1. What if an appropriate job aid could not be designed?

The company would have had to use a long and costly trial-and-error apprenticeship, accept the problem as unsolved, or try another consultant to design the job aid. (Several companies specialize in building job aids, so that option is realistic.) In this case, however, the trainer had taken a college-level course in the design of expert systems so it was not necessary to hire a consultant.

2. What if the trainees had been unable to learn the procedure?

If the trainees could not learn, it would be because the trainer (or the consulting company) was unable to design a job aid that was practical. Practicality implies that people otherwise qualified for the job can learn to use it.

3. Is it common to have difficulty designing the job aid?

Fortunately, a great many very useful job aids are easy to design. For example, most tasks to be performed by an entry-level worker can be job-aided without difficulty. On the other hand, estimating or market analysis or medical or psychiatric diagnosis are much more difficult to describe in a job aid.

4. What are the criteria for good job aids?

Job aids should be *simple, practical,* and *effective.*

- *Simplicity*: Job aids should be able to be used by people otherwise qualified to do a job. A job aid should contain no more than five items that must be kept in active memory at once.
- *Practicality*: A job aid must be in a form that can be used easily on the job. For example, a job aid laminated in plastic and placed in a visible place on a machine would be better in some environments than a more elegant computer-based job aid.
- *Effectiveness*: A job aid must be developed and tested to be sure that the person using it can do the task up to standard. For example, the time demands of a job might be such that the performer would not stop to use a job aid. If the aid fails to lead to good performance, it has not been adequately developed.

Because job aids come in many forms, expert job-aid designers have established specific standards for certain forms of job aids, e.g., size type for ease of reading at work stations, or amount of memory required for computer-assisted job aids.

5. When are job aids used?

A rule of thumb is that job aids should be the preferred instructional tool in performance-based instruction. First, design a job aid and, that failing, use some other instructional technique. The reason is simple: Job aids, properly developed, can often guide on-the-job performance so effectively that more expensive off-the-job training is not needed. A properly designed job aid can guide practice, enabling people to reach expert levels of performance with little wasted time.

How Performance-Based Job Aids Work

The procedure for designing job aids is very nearly the same as the procedure for doing on-the-job training as described in Chapter Two. The trainee observes the expert perform a task and writes a description of the performance standards and process to be used as a guide to learning how to do it. This description is a simple job aid. The purpose is to learn the job; in this case the job aid is a by-product and need not be elegant. On the other hand, when someone sets out to design a job aid, the purpose is to help others learn the job. The job-aid designer typically learns how to perform the task, but does not practice it to proficiency. The designer tests the job aid, however, by observing as other people use it.

Guided Observation

The first part of guided observation, learning why the job is important (what happens if it is done well? if it is done poorly?), was skipped in the estimator example. Trainees were already aware of the importance of doing the job well but had been unable to learn through on-the-job training.

The trainer's skill in analyzing work processes was greater than that of the typical learner, so the trainer was able to specify the process and design a job aid that enabled the trainees to learn the complex skills. The trainer's strategy for analyzing the job was to develop a prototype job aid and then ask the engineer to try to use it. The engineer found things that did not work and, at the same time, found ways to improve his own procedures. The improved procedures were incorporated into the job aid, which was then tested with a trainee. This job aid was complex (eventually taking the form of an expert system), but the process of prototyping and testing prototypes, first with experts and then with trainees, also works for simpler job aids.

Guided Practice

The trainees' first practice session was using the job aid to estimate. The estimates were real; this took less time for the expert and trainer than it would have taken to pull old estimates from the files and use them for practice. Practicing with real work also made the trainees feel more confident of their abilities and the expert feel that learning was occurring. As a side benefit, the expert claimed to have learned even more as a result of participating in the development of the job aid. That probably explained the expert's willingness to help develop the job aid.

Demonstration of Mastery

There were two difficulties in demonstrating mastery. The first was assuring that the trainee was tested with a full array of problems. The criterion of ten successful estimates was set to assure a reasonable range, but mastery would not be achieved if the trainee happened to have ten easy estimates in a row. The second problem was that estimates could be off for reasons beyond the estimator's control. The estimate might have been "right," but the order might have run over cost, been late, or been below quality standards because of unexpected changes in materials costs, illness of key production people, or simple human errors.

The first problem was easy to fix. The expert did not use consecutive orders for testing, but selected orders to assure that any set of ten contained the full range of possibilities. The trainee did consecutive orders for practice but did not know which ones were designated as "tests" by the expert.

The second problem was more difficult. The expert knew that no matter whose fault it was, if estimates were off, the company still risked loss of money or customers. That was the real-world standard, although it might not seem fair to the trainees. A "perfect" estimate that turns out to be wrong is still wrong. Thus, the solution was to acknowledge that incorrect estimates would occur and, rather than assign blame for any one error, the expert estimator worked with production people, etc., to track and decrease magnitude and frequency of errors. The expert's "errors" showed a slowly declining trend that set the goal and standard for the trainees: get your "error" trend progressively closer to the expert's trend!

Even an expert makes errors, but few will be within his or her control. The expert learns to factor into the estimates many of the potential glitches in making the product. The estimator had to learn about the production processes and likely problems over a long period on the job; the trainee learns that expertise through use of the job aid and therefore has a much faster learning curve.

Tips and Caveats

1. A job aid must be updated as changes in procedures occur. Although it is easier to update job aids than to retrain a work force using other methods, it is still necessary to do the updating. That is why it is good practice to ask new users of job aids for ideas about improving them. Not only are they likely to catch the procedural changes, but they bring a fresh perspective and might suggest ways of making significant improvements.

2. Many job aids have been designed, used successfully for a time, and then "lost." This typically happens because, after using a job aid for a time, people inter-

nalize it and do not need to refer to it. They quite literally lose the job aid and sometimes forget that it existed, thus never telling newcomers about it or showing them how to use it.

3. People have built very effective job aids for tasks that should no longer be done due to inattention to the "guided observation" step in which people learn why a task is performed.

4. Guided observation, per se, is not possible for new jobs or new tasks; paradoxically, the best time to build a job aid is for a new job. That is because designing the job and the job aid together assures that the job makes sense and can be learned readily by new people. (Many jobs and many tasks just happen in organizations. They are not designed, not logical, and sometimes not even necessary.)

5. It is not unusual for the expert's performance to improve as a result of being involved in the construction of a job aid. Experts tend to have several ways they can perform a task; some ways are better than others and even experts sometimes become a little sloppy. However, developing a job aid helps them to focus on their best performance rather than their worst performance or even their typical performance.

6. Each job aid an expert (or a novice) builds is considered complete only when users can readily master the task for which it is intended. Mastery in building job aids requires three things: evaluating the job aids (do they work?), building both simple and complex job aids, and reducing the amount of time it takes to build a job aid. The worksheet below can be used to track mastery of building job aids. Anyone fortunate enough to work with an expert job-aid builder will have a relatively rapid learning curve. There are also many good books about job aids and a few good training workshops. If you are considering attending one, ask to see some of the job aids graduates of the workshop have built.

Practice Exercises

Guided Observation Exercise One

Identify three job aids that are in use in your workplace. Look for simple checklists and recipelike job aids as well as more complex tools. Talk to people about them, asking questions such as:

- Why is the job aid used?
- What would happen if the job aid did not exist?
- How could the job aid be improved?

- What are some other job aids that might be useful, e.g., for difficult procedures, for infrequently used procedures, or to assure uniformity or high standards?

Guided Observation Exercise Two

If you find a job aid that could be improved, attempt to improve it and then interview the person using it to determine if it is better.

Guided Practice Exercise One

Make one or more of the following job aids:

- A map to your home
- A recipe for something good to eat
- A guide for preparing meals balanced among the major food groups
- A guide showing what cannot be said when interviewing a job applicant (or a guide showing what to say if someone asks you an inappropriate question when you are interviewing for a job)
- A step-by-step procedure for doing a simple work task (or convert the OJT documentation you did in Chapter Two into a job aid)

When you have made the job aid, test it twice, once by asking someone to read it aloud and tell you what he or she thinks it means, and once by asking someone to use it.

Guided Practice Exercise Two

Review the job aid in Figure 6.2. Pretend you are using it. Then make a job aid for a situation you choose, using the same format as the one shown.

Suggestion: When you make the job aid, do not try to be especially creative. Just select a topic that might be fun or useful and use the blank form, Figure 6.3.

You could select one of the following topics or use them for inspiration: the job interview material mentioned above, responding to requests people make of you at work, responding to objections as a salesperson, responding to unreasonable requests as part of assertiveness training, deciding which bills to pay this month, deciding who to ask to the Sadie Hawkins Dance or the senior prom or to your mother's for the weekend.

Comment: The Situation-Interpretation-Action format in Figure 6.3 is useful for a wide variety of interpersonal tasks. Supervisors, managers, trainers, and

FIGURE 6.2. ON-THE-SPOT JOB AID.

When is this job aid useful?

Whenever you want to know what to do when you are on the spot, e.g., in a meeting, conversation, presentation, or training session.

How should I use the job aid?

To guide practice before being put on the spot. (While you are on the spot you want to respond fluently rather than say, "Excuse me, I have to look at my script.")

Situation	Interpretation	Action
Someone asks you a direct question.	Your answer would not be well received.	Refer the question: position the group or an individual as an expert and ask the person or group "What do you think about that?"
	It's a trick question.	Reframe the question or split the question before answering, e.g., "Is this what you are asking . . . or is this . . . ?"
	It's a hostile question.	Reflect the feeling, e.g., "You sound troubled (or upset or . . .)" or "Are you upset with me about something?"
Someone dumps a complaint and acts as if you should do something.	There's something behind the complaint that you don't know about.	Use reflective listening: make eye contact, repeat a key phrase, and pause expectantly.
	The person wants you to "fix" it.	Ask a leading question, e.g., "What do you want me to do?" (Ask follow-up probing questions, e.g., "You know the situation. What could I do that would help?")
	You are not sure what to do.	Reflect, reframe, find something good to say about the complaint, then ask a leading question. Refer. (It's OK to refer it to yourself, e.g., "I don't have an answer now. I'll . . . and get back to you by . . .")
There's a long pause and eyes turn to you.	People want leadership.	Reflect what you've heard, ask for their ideas about next steps, then summarize, and ask if they agree.
	You feel you should say something.	Reflect, refer, reframe, or describe something good about the process; then ask for suggestions about next steps.

FIGURE 6.3. ON-THE-SPOT JOB AID (BLANK FORM).

When is this job aid useful?

How should I use the job aid?

Situation	Interpretation	Action

others go through a work day encountering a wide variety of critical situations. Each calls for action based on an interpretation of the situation. The Situation-Interpretation-Action format[1] is also useful for many technical tasks, e.g., determining which computer command to use for a particular task or which corrective action to take based on an SPC control chart pattern.

Guided Practice Exercise Three

Review the Audience-Centered Writing Process in Figure 6.4. It is intended for a person who can write business materials reasonably well but who tends to write without analyzing what the reader needs. Pretend that you are using it to write a specific business memo.

Make a job aid, using a flow chart format similar to Figure 6.5. This format is useful for a wide variety of procedures or tasks; in fact, it can be used for any

FIGURE 6.4. AUDIENCE-CENTERED WRITING PROCESS.

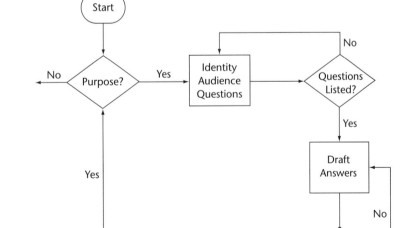

FIGURE 6.5. PERFORMANCE EPISODE CYCLE.

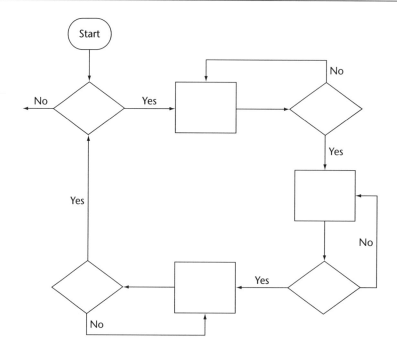

task that generates a product. Complex tasks always have a beginning phase, a middle phase, and a completion phase, so the format works as an overview of complex tasks. (Additional job aids can be constructed for the details of the phases.)

Guided Practice Exercise Four

Use the blank Performance Episode Cycle flow chart in Figure 6.5 to describe a task. Put the beginning step in the top rectangle, the middle step in the rectangle on the right side, and the ending step in the bottom rectangle. For example, the three steps might be "Establish Goal," "Design Intervention," and "Implement Intervention" or they might be "Greet Customer," "Identify Customer's Needs," and "Make Sales Presentation" or they might be "Sort Dirty Clothes," "Select Load to Wash," and "Start First Load." Each step leads to a yes/no decision point, e.g., "Boss accepts goal?," "Solution cost-effective?," and "Goal achieved?"

You might choose a task that describes the key part of a job and then use the job aid as part of the training for the job. You might also use the performance episode flow chart to describe one of the actions in a Situation-Interpretation-Action job aid. (When doing an S-I-A flow chart, it sometimes works to call the first rectangle "Interpret the Situation" and to begin the action in the second rectangle, reserving the third rectangle for the final step in the interaction. On the other hand, it sometimes, works better to use all three rectangles for the Action, assuming that the Interpretation was done at the decision point before the first rectangle. Analyzing performance into components is, to some extent, a trial-and-error process. That is one reason we should test the job aids to see if they will work the way we hope they will.)

Demonstration of Mastery

Having done the exercises above, you are a novice job-aid builder; becoming an expert requires considerable practice. Expert job-aid builders can quickly choose a format and then develop a job aid in that format. They do so by mastering one format at a time and designing new formats as needed. You might want to read some material on job aids, attend a workshop on building job aids, or go to the International Society for Performance Improvement's annual conference to mingle with job-aid users and experts. Should you choose to become expert in building job aids, that is the path to follow.

Note

1. The S-I-A format is inspired by Simpson's *Taxonomy for the Psychomotor Domain* (Simpson, 1961).

PART TWO

A PARADIGM FOR THE
TWENTY-FIRST CENTURY

CHAPTER SEVEN

PERFORMANCE-BASED INSTRUCTION: A PARADIGM FOR TWENTY-FIRST-CENTURY HUMAN RESOURCE DEVELOPMENT

An Overview

Where Are We Going?

This chapter is focused on the broad issues of performance-based instruction, different from the paradigm we have about instruction based on the experiences we had during elementary school and beyond. Performance-based instruction is different in important ways from most of the instruction we have experienced. This chapter covers the similarities and differences between performance-based instruction and traditional education or training.

- *Purpose*: An instructional paradigm guides HRD professionals through analysis, design, implementation, and evaluation of instruction. By comparing and contrasting the performance-based instruction paradigm with other paradigms, we learn more about the paradigms we use and can use them in a more appropriate manner.
- *Benefits*: Use of an appropriate paradigm can reduce design errors and make design more cost-effective. Using paradigms can assure that instructional programs with similar purposes have a similar look and feel.
- *Drawbacks*: A paradigm constrains. If an instructional paradigm is used, by plan or by default, for the wrong purpose it reduces the quality of instruction.

How Shall We Get There?

We will examine three paradigms, education, training, and performance-based instruction, to see where they differ in purpose:

- The *education paradigm* is that instruction is intended to transmit specific content; there is no responsibility for helping learners apply the content outside the classroom. Public education is designed to be of value to the learner, but not to prepare students for any specific vocation.
- The *training paradigm* is that instruction transmits content that is related to workplace performance; the trainer assumes responsibility for selecting content that is relevant to the workplace, but does not assume responsibility for helping learners use the content. Vocational education professionals and HRD professionals tend to illustrate the training paradigm.
- The *performance-based instruction paradigm* is that instruction enables people to perform competently in the workplace; it assumes responsibility for relevance, applicability, and application of the content. Many educators and trainers use performance-based instruction techniques, but few use them consistently.

We will analyze the three paradigms in context to see how each developed and how each serves us in today's training environment. After some tips and caveats, we will provide some guided observation and practice exercises to provide further understanding of the paradigms.

How Will We Know We've Arrived?

Readers are invited to use the following self-assessment checklist after completing the chapter:

Self-Assessment Checklist
- How does the purpose of each paradigm influence the instructional methods and content?
- What are some of the reasons performance-based instruction is more difficult to use in the public education system than in the working world?
- What are some places in which performance-based instruction is, or could be, used in the public education system?
- Why do students enjoy classes related to the performing arts, e.g., music, dance, theater, physical education? What elements of performance-based instruction are typically present in the performing arts?
- How could mastery demonstrations in academic subjects be made to resemble mastery demonstrations in the performing arts?

- What are some training programs that most resemble educational programs? What training programs most resemble performance-based instruction?
- How could "educationlike" training programs be made more like performance-based instruction?
- How could English composition be taught using performance-based instruction?
- How could business math be taught using performance-based instruction?
- How could basic arithmetic be taught using performance-based instruction?
- How could basic literacy skills be taught using performance-based instruction?
- How does performance-based instruction relate to principles of adult learning?

Another indication of success will be the ability to use the three paradigms in practical ways:

- *Guided Observation*: HRD professionals can use knowledge of paradigms to evaluate training designs: What method is appropriate? What method is being used? Does it match the purpose? Is it being properly used?
- *Guided Practice*: HRD professionals can use their knowledge of the three educational paradigms to decide exactly why they are using a particular one, to choose more carefully the methods of instruction, and to guide clients and others toward appropriate methods.
- *Demonstration of Mastery*: HRD professionals show mastery by avoiding design errors from mismatching purpose and method and by successfully guiding clients in their selections.

An Educational Paradigm Example

Most public and private education courses are, not surprisingly, examples of the education paradigm. Public school children are taught about the world that lies beyond things they have seen and beyond the practical or playful things they do every day. Because much of the curriculum is intended to move the children beyond their everyday experience, teachers often do lessons that are similar to guided observation. They read stories that take children to imaginary lands, they show movies, dramatize, and prepare exhibits. One of teachers' main tasks, in fact, is bringing materials into the classroom that enable children to learn experientially or by observation. Teachers also have students do projects that result in specific products, e.g., a science fair exhibit or a collection of poems from different cultures. But the adult-learning principle of immediate applicability is achieved much less often than many teachers, parents, and children would like. Saying to students, "You can do it when you're older!" provides weak consolation for them in learning things they do not need now or in preventing them from digging more deeply into subjects they may wish to pursue.

Vocational education and most training courses seem more applicable. Examples of the performance-based instruction paradigm are found in the performing or practical arts such as industrial arts, home economics, or physical education. If we learn to plan a menu or a meeting or cook a casserole or make a lamp, we have, at least, a tangible product with which to demonstrate mastery. The Suzuki method of piano instruction is also very similar to performance-based instruction.

Much of the content of both vocational and training courses is intended to have practical applications. Vocational students go in many directions when they graduate; we hope that they are prepared for whatever they might encounter and include some extra material "just in case." The same is true of many training courses. Not knowing what is really needed back on the job, the trainer cannot tailor the programs, even though they try. Students often perceive a rather murky connection between what they are being asked to learn and what they might be doing later on. The performance-based instruction paradigm asks HRD professionals to take on the burden of making the connections.

Figure 7.1 illustrates the similarities and differences among the three paradigms. They are similar in that each is intended to facilitate learning. They differ in (1) the reasons for facilitating learning, (2) the roles of learners and teachers, and (3) the major benefits of the learning. The purposes of public education are broad and admirable. The purposes of vocational education or training are broad and practical. The purposes of performance-based instruction are narrow and practical.

Analysis of Paradigms

1. Why do we need a new paradigm?

Neither the public nor vocational education paradigm takes full responsibility for transfer of training. That requires moving out of classrooms and into workplaces to forge linkages to workplace performance. Fulfilling the responsibility for transfer of training requires a three-way partnering among:

- People responsible for the instruction
- People responsible for workplace performance
- People responsible for learning

FIGURE 7.1. OVERVIEW OF THREE INSTRUCTIONAL PARADIGMS.

	General Education	Vocational Education	Training
Paradigm	Content-Based Instruction	Performance-Related Instruction	Performance-Based Instruction
Purpose	Transmit cultural heritage	Transmit useful knowledge	Develop valuable performance
Models	Oral tradition	Apprenticeship	Master performer
Methods	Present, test, and promote those who pass tests	Present, guide practice, test, and certify people who pass tests	Demonstrate, guide practice, provide feedback, and certify competence
Content	Knowledge first: selected with deference to academic subject matter experts, social philosophers, publishers	Skills first: selected with deference to practitioner subject matter experts	Content secondary: selected with deference to accomplished performers
Teacher's role and preparation	Authority/evaluator, presenter; extensive content preparation plus brief instruction in methods	Mentor, presenter, evaluator; extensive content preparation plus experience plus brief instruction in methods	Coach; experience in facilitating adult learning
Student's role and preparation	Recipient of truth; prerequisite courses	Recipient of useful information; prerequisite courses	Novice performer acquiring mastery; acquisition of learning skills
Scheduling	By clock and calendar with consideration of administrative needs	By clock and calendar with consideration of instructional needs	By instructional needs with consideration of clock and calendar
Problems	Enormity of scope. Time lags between learning and use. Integration of parts and wholes. Lock step.	Breadth of scope. Time lags between learning and use. Integration of parts and wholes. Changing technology. Cost.	Narrowness of focus Integration of parts and wholes. Cost.

2. What is wrong with the old paradigms?

The flaw is not with the public education paradigm or the vocational education paradigm per se; each has its place and its limitations. The flaw occurs if we attempt to use methods for purposes they were never intended to fulfill. Public education simply is not intended to prepare people for the workplace—though it is intended to provide people with the skills of reading, writing, computing, and reasoning that would help them to be successful there. Vocational education is not intended to train people for the needs of a specific workplace; it seeks to provide people with marketable skills that could be used in a variety of workplaces. Training, as purchased from vendors, tends not to focus on a specific workplace; training, as developed internally, often leaves transfer up to the learners.

Instruction patterned after either of the educational paradigms just does not achieve specific workplace goals. Ideally, both contribute general knowledge and skills that performance-based instruction can build on to meet the challenges of the workplace.

3. What relation is this to the distinctions HRD makes among education, training, and development?

Human resource professionals have described education as having broad aims (e.g., to transmit a culture) and training as having a more narrow aim (to provide knowledge, skills, and attitudes relevant to the workplace). Similarly, the authors have contrasted training (aimed at current workplace needs) with development (aimed at future workplace needs). Performance-based instruction *includes* development. Performance-based instruction focuses on *improving* workplace performance, not simply on teaching people knowledge, skills, and attitudes that relate in some general way to the workplace. Performance-based training either eliminates "nice to know" material or shows why it is important and when and how to use it. Similarly, performance-based training includes very little "just in case" material except as job aids.

Performance-based instruction emphasizes training that improves performance now and positions for the future, assuring that both training and development occur. For example, a manager who needs a stronger financial background for a future promotion might incorporate advanced financial analysis techniques in current budget planning or might volunteer to serve on a task force dealing with integrating financial strategies in business operations. Both tactics would help him or her improve current performance and, at the same time, develop so that he or she could take on the promotion.

4. Where did the vocational education paradigm start?

Vocational education probably emerged as young people observed older people doing important tasks. Learning at a mother's or father's knee enabled children to acquire valuable skills—and it still does. Children also learned trades by watching and helping other adults long before such arrangements became formalized as apprenticeships. Vocational education was a logical step forward, formalizing what had previously been done informally. If someone taught several children at once, then it was vocational education.

5. Where did the public education paradigm start?

Public education grew out of the stories elders told, i.e., out of the oral tradition. The stories often had a moral that related to living one's life in the company of others. Probably the first formalized educational process came in the form of religious education. Story telling evolved into lecturing and informal sessions evolved into scheduled classes on scheduled topics. Children were expected to learn what was taught, often verbatim. It was the job of the school to teach the words, and the job of the parents and community to assure that the children lived in accordance with the teachings.

6. Where did the performance-based paradigm come from?

Before vocational education was formalized, it probably followed the performance-based instruction paradigm very closely. Children observed a variety of adults and observed more closely those whose performance interested them the most. They imitated and the expert probably gave a few pointers. If the novice practiced some more and grew better, the interest of both the novice and the expert was maintained and the coaching continued. Eventually, the novice mastered enough tasks to begin helping the expert, perhaps taking over the work as the expert retired.

Formal vocational education took on broader goals rather than the task of preparing one person for a specific job. As vocational pursuits created leisure and the opportunity to learn something more than was necessary to earn a living, public education received more attention.

Now, we are rediscovering performance-based instruction, as HRD professionals have been influenced, either negatively or positively, by the instruction they have experienced, usually in school. The instructional models we have experienced have served as a model for the education paradigm. Courses in vocational education were not held in high enough esteem and courses in the performing arts were outside the mainstream.

People encountered courses in public or vocational education that just did not work very well. As HRD professionals, they sought to avoid some of the flaws and reject much of what they had experienced as children, labeling it pedagogy. HRD professionals have long attempted to make training relevant to the job. The performance-based instruction paradigm is consistent with HRD aspirations and attempts to make instruction relevant to the needs of adult learners. It provides a rationale that legitimatizes what HRD professionals do and contrasts our charge with that of public and vocational education. Their purposes are quite different from those of the modern HRD professional.

7. Could the performance-based instruction paradigm be used for public and vocational education?

Just as a journey is completed one step at a time, learning occurs one step at a time. The knowledge, skills, and attitudes we seek to transmit in public education could be learned through performance-based instruction. For example, public education seeks to liberate through knowledge; reading, writing, and computation are especially liberating and can be acquired through performance-based instruction. Similarly, learning to learn is at the heart of public education. However, current statistics suggest that most do not acquire that coveted ability; it can, however, be acquired, reliably, through performance-based instruction.

How the Paradigm Works

We know much more about how learning takes place now than we did. We also know much more about what it takes to support excellent performance in the workplace than we did. The performance-based instruction paradigm incorporates these two relatively new areas of knowledge, adult learning (Knowles, 1984, 1986) and performance theory (Gilbert, 1996; Langdon, 1995; Rummler & Brache, 1995).

Guided Observation

Learners, during the guided observation phase, see for themselves why, what, and how: Why is what they are learning important? What does it accomplish? How is it done? This relates directly to adult motivation and sets up adult learning. By letting the learners see for themselves and make up their own minds, performance-based instruction treats learners as intelligent beings. It also keeps the designer honest; if we can show convincing evidence about *why, what,* and *how,* we can be sure that the instruction is relevant to the workplace. If we cannot show such evidence, we can at least honestly acknowledge that we cannot justify the instruction within the public or vocational education paradigms.

Guided Practice

Learners call upon their prior knowledge during guided practice. The guided observation links the learning to the workplace; the guided practice links the learning to the prior knowledge, skills, and attitudes the learners bring. The practice is guided to allow for an interplay between the knowledge learners bring and the performance requirements of the workplace. The facilitation process treats prior learning with respect, supports workplace requirements, and coaches learners to use what works and set aside what does not.

Demonstration of Mastery

Performance-based instruction is meant to achieve high standards of workplace performance, identified as objectively as possible. In combination with guided observation, which establishes motivation, and guided practice, which supports adult learning, demonstration of mastery supports and develops competence, self-respect, and confidence. The modern workplace would benefit greatly from increased competence, self-respect, and confidence.

Tips and Caveats

1. Performance-based courses can be found in both public education and vocational education settings. Some trainers unconsciously use the paradigm they have experienced in school; some instructors in public education settings use the performance-based instruction paradigm. The instructional techniques, as well as the analysis, design, and evaluation that go into them, are what define performance-based instruction.
2. Performance is both product and process. The performance-based instruction achieves its focus and relevance by attention to products; it achieves excellence only when it teaches processes that reliably yield excellent products. It is not a focus on product that makes it work and it is not a focus on process that makes it work, but both.
3. Performance is both product and process. Performance-based instruction focuses on a product, e.g., a paragraph or a limerick or a shoe or a coaching plan or a business plan or a research proposal or a clock or a subassembly or a completed sales slip or a review of a play or a budget or a properly arranged merchandise display. If we can identify a product, identify good products and not-so-good products, and identify a process that yields good products, we can use performance-based instruction. We can teach people to use the process to produce the product.

Practice Exercises

Guided Observation Exercises

Do one or more of the following:

1. Think of one or two of the best courses you have taken in school. Then think of one or two of the worst courses you have taken there. Using Figure 7.1 as a guide, which paradigm did the best courses most closely resemble? Which paradigm did the worst course most closely resemble?
2. Do the same for training courses you have designed or taken.
3. Do the same for any courses you have taken to learn a skill, such as swimming, first aid, cooking, or dog training.

Guided Practice Exercise One

1. Make a blank graph with the same rows and columns as Figure 7.1.
2. Think about a good performance-related course or training program you have taken; describe the course, filling in the Performance-Related column.
3. Describe how it might be if it were a Content-Based course.
4. Now describe how it might be if it were a Performance-Based course.
5. Discuss the three versions of the course with a colleague. What is good about each version? Why is the Performance-Based course better for some purposes?

Guided Practice Exercise Two

1. Make another blank graph, patterned after Figure 7.1.
2. Determine if there is a Content-Based course you might want to convert to Performance-Based. Describe it, first, in the Content-Based column.
3. Describe the course as it would be if it were Performance-Related.
4. Describe the course as it would be if it were Performance-Based.
5. Discuss the three versions of the course with a colleague. Would it be feasible to convert it to a Performance-Based course? Would it be better to convert it, first, to a Performance-Related course and then, over time, convert it to a Performance-Based course?

Guided Practice Exercise Three

1. Show Figure 7.1 to a prospective client. Alternatively, or in addition, show the specific variants of it that you have generated to describe specific courses.
2. Discuss the paradigms. Ask the client specific questions about it, such as: "Which of the three purposes is most important to you?" "Why?" "Which of the Models and Methods seem most appropriate to you for this setting?" "Which student role fits this setting best?" Prepare the questions in advance.

3. Close the discussion with the pros and cons of moving toward performance-related instruction for some courses and performance-based instruction for courses that are especially important.

Demonstrations of Mastery Exercises

Mastery of the performance-based instruction paradigm occurs gradually as you gain experience with it, but there are a number of clues that tell you how you are doing. Every six months or so, you might stop and reflect:

1. Notice the extent to which you feel more confident about using performance-based instruction after having compared the three paradigms.
2. Notice the extent to which you can discuss performance-based instruction more readily, now that you can compare it with the other two paradigms.
3. Notice whether or not you can describe the advantages of the performance-based instruction paradigm without feeling as if you are criticizing the other paradigms.
4. Notice whether doing performance-based instruction becomes more natural to you as you use it more. If you begin finding it difficult to do other forms of instruction because performance-based instruction seems better to you, it is a sign that you have mastered the paradigm well enough to use it when the situation calls for it.

CHAPTER EIGHT

CONVERTING TO PERFORMANCE-BASED INSTRUCTION

An Overview

Where Are We Going?

Much workplace instruction is very good at increasing awareness, orienting, informing, and providing potentially useful knowledge. However, performance-based instruction (PBI) focuses on what traditional instruction has done well occasionally but not consistently: improving performance. This chapter shows how to convert existing instruction to performance-based instruction.

- *Purpose*: Converting existing instruction to performance-based instruction enables HRD professionals to use the best of what already exists, adding value by focusing on performance.
- *Benefits*: Converting existing instruction saves developmental costs, reduces lead time, and adds to the workplace value of training. The conversion process can pay for itself through reducing trainee time and improving the value added through performance improvement.
- *Drawbacks*: Converting to performance-based instruction alters the relationship between HRD and HRD customers; the change can be uncomfortable. In addition, there is typically no mandate from upper levels of management to make the change; if they did not ask for it, they are more likely to resist than to reward the change.

How Shall We Get There?

We recommend a practical process that uses much of the existing instruction, at least at first, doing the conversion as a continuous-improvement project. The conversion occurs one piece at a time—a unit or lesson or exercise. For example, we might begin by adding an action-planning lesson, perhaps deleting outdated material. The revised instruction typically follows the guided observation and practice to mastery model.

- *Guided Observation*: Learners are shown examples of good and not-so-good performance. They learn to identify the difference between good and not-so-good processes and products or results. For example, in a workshop on win-win negotiating, people would first learn whether or not a negotiated agreement is really a win for both parties and, second, they would learn to identify successful and self-defeating negotiating procedures.
- *Guided Practice*: Learners practice, with goals and feedback. For example, they would practice effective negotiating procedures and tactics for early detection and correction of self-defeating procedures. They might role play until they were at ease with successful negotiations and then practice with real but low-risk and low-difficulty negotiations until they were successful.
- *Demonstration of Mastery*: Learners practice until they can do simulated or real tasks that meet the standards required by each situation. For example, in the win-win negotiation lesson, the trainer would arrange for on-the-job coaching and monitoring for everyone. The standard of mastery would be tailored to the individual, i.e., people doing win-win negotiating as a tactic for accomplishing work within the organization would not set as stringent a standard as those negotiating major contracts or major disputes.

How Will We Know We've Arrived?

The reader is invited to determine understanding of the conversion process—why it is done and how it is done—by use of the following self-assessment checklist:

> ### *Self-Assessment Checklist*
> - How can inserting more action planning or applications projects into a good non-performance-based course make it better?
> - What would be hardest for you about converting to PBI?
> - How can documented success stories be used to show people where they are going and how they will get there?

- How can following up with former trainees to discover their successes in application help in converting to PBI?
- How can documented success stories be obtained and used to help people prepare prior to a course so they get more out of it?
- What are some of the advantages of converting gradually?
- How could applications exercises be added to an interpersonal skills course (e.g., effective listening, effective negotiations) to make it more performance-based? How do you think that would change the effectiveness of the course?

There are several practice exercises at the end of the chapter. Each exercise enables learners to assess mastery of specific skills or knowledge and guides them toward ever increasing mastery of the conversion process and of performance-based instruction.

Example of a Coaching Seminar

A coaching seminar had been developed in a large corporation (over $3 billion annual sales) based on an outstanding book, *Coaching for Improved Work Performance* (Fournies, 1978), and was considered successful by the training staff and by participants. The training manager believed that the impact of the seminar could be improved by converting it to a performance-based instruction workshop.

Guided Observation

The newly converted workshop begins with examples of successful coaching projects, showing the steps in the coaching process and the results/products of each step. Participants review the examples and examples from their own experience. They analyze the examples, both successful and unsuccessful, to identify critical success factors. The guided observation phase concludes with a description of the coaching process, made specific, practical, and useful by casting it in the form of a blank worksheet that becomes a coaching plan when filled in.

Guided Practice

Each participant develops a coaching plan to achieve a specific result with a specific person. For example, a participant might coach a staff member about a performance problem such as chronic tardiness, frequent errors, or misreading customer needs. Another participant might coach an otherwise excellent performer about the person's inability to work effectively with others. A third participant might develop a plan for coaching upward to help a boss be more specific when delegating or to help a boss keep staff meetings productive rather than drifting.

The workshop sessions occur once a week for two hours. Participants develop steps for a coaching plan and implement them between sessions. For example, participants may plan a coaching interaction in which they will work with an individual to define a performance goal to be achieved. They role play the coaching interaction until they are ready to try it, then perform the step between workshop sessions and report back in the next session.

Demonstration of Mastery

Each weekly workshop session begins with an evaluation of the coaching participants have done between sessions. Participants report what worked well and what did not. Participants then work together to come up with ideas for implementing the next step of the plan or for recycling a previous step.

Overall mastery is evaluated in terms of criteria established for each coaching plan, tailored to the specific situation but always including win-win-win criteria. In other words, benefits to the person being coached, to the coach, and to the corporation.

Analysis of the Example

1. Is practice with only one coaching plan too limited for mastery of the coaching skills?

Participants begin with some degree of mastery—they are not total novices—and improve their coaching skills. They obtain additional practice as they work with other participants and see several examples of coaching plans and practice through role plays with other participants. They say (on evaluations) that the improvement is significant.

Of course, they are not as good at coaching as they will become with more practice, but they obtain better results from their coaching than participants did before the conversion. In addition, the HRD staff support the continued practice. The trainer provides follow-up coaching and encourages participants to meet periodically to go over their progress. Additional coaching workshops are offered, focused on topics such as coaching of groups or coaching in team building providing further opportunities to practice the coaching skills.

2. How can one coaching plan fit so many different situations?

The plan is set up in several broad phases, much the way a general problem-solving process is set up. Several specific questions must be answered in each phase and the answers are tailored to the situation, for example: "How will the person you are coaching respond when . . . ?" and "How did the person you are coaching respond when . . . ?"

3. How did participants react to the change to a performance-based workshop?

Some complain about having to come to several sessions. They want to come to a half-day session, learn all about coaching, and go back to work able to solve all the problems they encounter. On the other hand, most people, even those who complain, recognize that they get more out of the workshop than they would have with a different design.

Some complain about having to work. They want to come to a training session that is fun and relaxing, providing a break from work. The term "workshop" is taken quite literally in performance-based instruction. Participants do actual and productive work during the session. It is not a vacation, contrary to the expectations built up over the years in some organizations.

On the other hand, complaints are mild and offered with humor. We believe that is because the original seminar was a good one, because the conversion was gradual, and because the trainer develops a good relationship with participants.

4. What is the major difference between the seminar and the workshop?

The major difference is that everything focuses on the coaching plan in the workshop; participants had been encouraged to plan applications at the seminar, but that had not been an organizing focus.

5. Can traditional instruction be converted to performance-based instruction in all settings?

Performance-based instruction—or something very close to it—is common in elementary and secondary schools in extra-curricular activities such as sports and forensics and in elective courses such as band, home economics, and industrial arts. It is also used in colleges and universities in both graduate and undergraduate courses, but primarily in graduate courses.[1]

How the Conversion Process Works

Converting to performance-based instruction is an exercise in reengineering or reinventing. The designer goes through an orderly *analysis, design, implement, and evaluate* process. Figure 8.1 shows the analysis phase in two parts, a business needs analysis that generates a Specification of Business Needs and a performance analysis that generates a Specification of Performance Requirements. The design phase

FIGURE 8.1. TWO STRATEGIES FOR DEVELOPING PERFORMANCE-BASED INSTRUCTION.

Phases	Ideal Strategy	Bootstrap Strategy
Specification of Business Need	Develop broadly based agreement on documented current or strategic need or specific business result.	In absence of agreement on current or strategic need/result, make intelligent guesses.
Specification of Performance Requirements	• Specify performance products that will lead to desired result. • Specify quality criteria for each product. • Identify master performers for each product. • Identify processes for each product, neatly described by flow charts defining sets of sub-products that can be generated by sets of manageable tasks.	• Make intelligent guesses about performance products, processes, and performers. • Create product specifications and quality criteria. • Create process flow charts. • Create subproducts and component tasks. • Persuade someone to try out the new processes and refine them until they work reasonably well.
Designing Performance-Based Instruction	• Obtain examples of excellent and acceptable products. • Obtain examples of products deficient in key ways. • Arrange demonstrations of excellent and acceptable processes. • Identify subproducts and related processes. • Continue breaking processes into parts to identify tasks that can be accomplished by novice performers.	• Obtain messy examples and modify them or create useful examples. • Create simulations of processes. • Create processes from tasks that can be accomplished by novice performers if they are given simple tools and the easiest forms of the tasks.
Implementing and Evaluating Performance-Based Instruction	• Developmentally test and revise instructional tasks until learners meet performance criteria. • Assist learners as needed to incorporate tasks into performance.	• Developmentally test instructional tasks until learners meet some of the criteria. • Modify design of tasks until they can be tested on the job. • Continue modifying job design and instructional tasks until levels of performance are agreed on and achieved.

is next, followed by the implement and evaluate phases. The figure shows two strategies for developing performance-based instruction, an ideal strategy and a bootstrap strategy.

The bootstrap strategy is illustrated below to show how it was used in reengineering the coaching seminar.

- *Specification of Business Need*: The corporation is active in both domestic and international markets, expanding in numbers of products as well as numbers of countries in which the products are distributed. It is a safe guess that a significant business issue is how to bring people up to speed quickly as directions change to meet frequently changing demands.
- *Specification of Performance Requirements*: Bringing people up to speed quickly, frequently, and in many different environments will place demands on all parts of the corporation. Managers throughout the corporation will need to be good at coaching the people who work within their spheres of influence and responsibility. The question facing the instructional designer was how to design instruction tailored to the mind-boggling variety of needed accomplishments throughout the corporation. The approach taken in the original seminar was to teach the skills and leave the tailoring up to each of the hundreds of persons who might eventually receive the instruction. Performance-based instruction requires a different focus on the specific coaching performance of each manager.
- *Design*: The first, and probably the most difficult, step in converting to performance-based instruction was deciding what product master coaches produce. A great coach attracts great athletes and prepares them to win contests, but what is the product of the coaching itself? Not "a winning season"; that is a result of the whole organization. Not "improved performance"; that is the result of the interaction between the great coach and the performer. What is the tangible product? The designer decided that the product had to be a coaching plan, even though expert coaches do not always commit their coaching plans to paper; novices, on the other hand, would benefit from thinking things through on paper until the planning process became automatic.
- *Implement/Evaluate*: An important part of implementing the performance-based design was to decide on quality standards for each part of the coaching plan. The criteria emerged as the designer/instructor looked at many better and worse examples generated by participants and facilitated discussions among participants about what worked in their workplaces. The participants were partners in setting effective performance criteria. As the criteria emerged, it became much easier to guide practice toward mastery.

Guided Observation

The reengineering project was on-the-job training and development for the trainer. The seven differences between performance-based and other instruction (shown in Figure 8.2) told the trainer what to look for.

- *Purpose*: How can I refocus from teaching them about coaching to helping them use coaching to improve performance in their work units?
- *Models*: Where can I find actual examples of exemplary coaching in this setting?
- *Method*: How can I help them to see examples of excellent coaching and arrange for the guided practice and feedback?
- *Instructor's Role*: How can I change my role to minimize presentations and provide more guided practice?
- *Learner's Role*: How can I deal with learners' expectations and long history of being relatively passive recipients of knowledge and make it safe for them to move into a partnering role?

 FIGURE 8.2. FEATURES OF PERFORMANCE-BASED AND OTHER INSTRUCTION.

Feature	Performance-Based Instruction	Other Instruction
1. Purpose	To improve workplace performance.	To provide knowledge, skills, or attitudes.
2. Models of Excellence	Performance of best (exemplary) performers	Knowledge of subject matter experts
3. Methods	*Guided Observation and Practice:* demonstrations of exemplary products of performance and processes for generating products; guided practice with feedback.	*Presentations and Discussions:* present and discuss knowledge, skill, and attitudes to be acquired.
4. Instructor's Role	*Coach:* individualize practice, debrief demonstrations and exercises, support high standards of performance.	*Presenter:* present information well, keep to the schedule.
5. Learner's Role	*Active partner:* select applications, do tasks, accept guidance.	*Recipient of knowledge:* accept what is offered; memorize content.
6. Scheduling	Flexible to assure that on-the-job performance occurs during or immediately after training.	Rigid, dictated by clock and calendar.
7. Evaluation	Answers questions such as: How well does performance match organizational needs? How well do conditions of learning match conditions of performance? How much did performance improve?	Answers questions such as: How much information is presented? How well is the information presented? How much knowledge was acquired?

- *Scheduling*: How can I move from the convenience of a one-or two-session training event to a schedule that provides adult learners an opportunity to test the content by trying it in the workplace?
- *Evaluating*: How can I help participants to evaluate their own coaching attempts so that they can learn the skills and continuously improve?

Guided Practice

Each time the trainer found an opportunity to make the changes in instructional purposes, methods, etc., he or she could practice the skills involved in making the changes. The gradual change, necessitated by the fact than the trainer had little time and energy available to "fix" the seminar (when it was not broken), also made it possible for the trainer to practice the new skills, evaluate them, and improve them.

Demonstration of Mastery

Mastery was reflected in the improved results participants achieved with their coaching projects. Their increased mastery also demonstrated the trainer's increased mastery.

Tips and Caveats

1. Specifying performance requirements (see Figure 8.1) requires identifying performance products, not an easy task when the performers are knowledge workers, managers, and professionals. Much of their work might not produce tangible products, especially when the performer has done the work for years and is an expert at it. It is sometimes useful to invent a tangible product. The coaching plan in the example above is such a product; completed analysis worksheets and progress reports are other commonly used products.
2. Converting to performance-based instruction cannot be accomplished overnight. The HRD staff, their clients, and upper-level management typically must change their mind-sets about the role and function of training. A traditional training department might have been the place to send people to be fixed, but a human resource development department that is worthy of the name has a different function. Human resource development is best accomplished in partnership. Performance-based instruction requires a team effort; building teamwork requires guided practice.
3. HRD professionals with little or no experience with performance-based instruction can acquire experience through a series of small, low-risk proj-

ects in which they convert existing instruction. There are three ways to minimize risks:

- Begin by gradually converting a successful course (modeling continuous improvement).
- Convert an important course that is clearly in trouble (modeling responsiveness to customers).
- Add performance-based application exercises near the end of a few existing courses.

4. Some people who complete non-performance-based education or training courses and workshops do, in fact, use what they have learned to improve workplace performance. Find out how they do it and begin presenting their successes as examples. (This tactic was very helpful in reengineering the coaching seminar.)

5. Training vendors often do traditional instruction well. An HRD staff can add performance-based application exercises, thereby supporting and adding value to the courses purchased from them.

6. Some training vendors want to offer performance-based instruction and have the expertise to do so, but they have not been able to sell it. Many organizations find it expedient to send people to courses in the hope they will be "fixed"; it works for some of the people some of the time—in the authors' experience, a very good traditional training course works for 10–20 percent of the people who attend. However, many training vendors would be happy to partner with in-house HRD professionals to develop performance-based instruction. Of course, the buyer must beware, as some very well known vendors claim to offer performance-based instruction but actually offer traditional instruction in new binders.

7. OJT is a great place to start educating an organization about performance-based instruction. So, too, is team building or problem solving or cost reduction or technical writing. Computer utilization is also a good place to start in companies without information systems departments or data processing departments that guard that turf.

Practice Exercises

Guided Observation Exercises

Do one or more of the following exercises.

1. For a training session you have attended, review the experience and identify opportunities for converting parts of it to performance-based instruction. If

you have successfully applied something from the session, consider that as a potential application exercise; if you are planning to apply something from the session, consider how the project might have been set up as an applications exercise.

2. For a training session you will attend soon, talk with your boss or colleagues about things you might do in your work based on what you hope to learn. Design an application project. The project might become part of your developmental plan (see Chapter Four).

3. For a training session to which you plan to send someone, talk with the person about things that he or she might do based on what you hope will be learned. Prepare a draft of an application project now and meet with the person after the session to refine or revise the application plan.

4. For a training session you have recently run, interview some of the people who attended. Ask questions about applications they have made. Work with them to identify potential applications.

5. For a training session you plan to run soon, review it to identify one to three opportunities for revising existing lessons or exercises to focus on applications. (Use Figure 8.1 or Figure 8.2 to help guide this review.) Interview participants informally before and during the session. Discuss possible applications.

6. Interview would-be training vendors about their willingness to partner with you in customizing performance-based instruction.

Guided Practice Exercises

1. Follow through with one or more of the opportunities you identify (through the Guided Observation exercises or in some other way).

2. Pick a low-risk opportunity (see Tips and Caveats, number 2) for converting all or part of a course to performance-based instruction. Use Figure 8.1 as a guide and begin reengineering the course.

Demonstration of Mastery Exercise

Give some thought to how you might use what you know about converting existing instruction to performance-based instruction. If you do a lot of work in this area, you might design a summary tracking chart similar to Figure 8.3 to measure your progress in converting to performance-based instruction and, in the process, obtain information about the added value of doing so.

FIGURE 8.3. DEMONSTRATIONS OF MASTERY.

Project	Goal	Start	End	Comments/Results

Note

1. The Learning-to-Learn® system described in Chapter Thirteen is taught as a performance-based undergraduate course in many colleges and universities.

CHAPTER NINE

TRANSFER OF TRAINING: LINKING TO WHAT HAPPENS BEFORE AND AFTER

An Overview

Where Are We Going?

Training can be seen as the means of forging a link between a learner's prior knowledge, skills, and attitudes and the realities and demands of the workplace. An essential aspect of performance-based instruction is to assure that what people learn is used on the job. This chapter provides techniques to improve the impact of training, and, of course, techniques to "do it right the first time" as we develop new training events.

- *Purpose*: We link instruction to learner and organization to facilitate learning and assure that both learners and organization benefit.
- *Benefits*: Making specific connections to the past and future facilitates adult learning, reduces extraneous material, assures applicability, and optimizes training costs and benefits.
- *Drawbacks*: Making the connections is sometimes difficult because people in the workplace do not know what performance is needed, so it is impossible for them to establish effective performance-support or performance-management systems. As a result, many performance systems have deficiencies that should be addressed prior to or during the training event. Addressing performance-support system defects is a traditional role of industrial engineering and

supervision; addressing management-system defects is a traditional role of middle and upper management. Addressing such defects is neither a traditional nor an expected role for HRD professionals. However, if the deficiencies are not addressed, the positive impacts of training will be much less than optimal.

How Shall We Get There?

We will cover an orderly process for designing performance-based instruction so that what is learned transfers to the workplace. Designers of performance-based instruction identify relevant linkages by analysis on the front end, establishing the linkages during the training, and forging the linkages through follow-up support. The linkages are formed, not in the designer's office, but by partnering with people in the workplace.

The example will illustrate seven key linkages that must be in place to support adult learning and transfer to the workplace. After some tips and caveats, we will present several practice exercises to help the learner become proficient at designing properly linked instruction and at modifying existing instruction to improve linkages.

How Will We Know We've Arrived?

We are successful when the linkages are formed. The evaluation checklist in Figure 9.1 will help assess whether instruction has been linked to the workplace.

Readers are invited to use the following self-assessment checklist to assess understanding of the importance and process of linking training events to the workplace:

Self-Assessment Checklist
- How do examples taken directly from the workplace facilitate learning and transfer?
- How can performance data from the workplace help to describe the goals of training, show the importance of guided practice, and establish realistic standards for mastery?
- What are some ways that linkages between training events and the workplace facilitate adult learning?
- If a person, fresh from training, says "That's not the way we learned in training," what are two or three likely responses from peers or people with positions of authority? (The answers are different depending on

FIGURE 9.1. DO LINKAGES TO WORKPLACE SUPPORT TRANSFER OF TRAINING?

Linkage	Evaluation Questions	Answer/Estimate
1. Goal or Mission	Is it clear to learners how the organization and the learner would benefit if the material were learned well?	Yes, maybe, maybe not, no
2. Inputs: Instructional Content	Is "nice-to-know" or "just-in-case" material minimized and "use-it-now" material emphasized?	Yes, maybe, maybe not, no
3. Instructional Processes	Are learners given adequate guided observation so they can answer why, what, and how questions?	Yes, maybe, maybe not, no
	Are the answers to Mager's questions apparent to learners throughout instruction?	Yes, maybe, maybe not, no
4. Outputs: Learner Products	Do learner products during instruction match work products?	Yes, maybe, maybe not, no
	Do learner processes during guided practice match workplace processes?	Yes, maybe, maybe not, no
	Do performance standards during mastery match performance standards in the workplace?	Yes, maybe, maybe not, no
5. Feedback During Instruction	Do learners receive enough (guiding, supportive, nonpunishing) feedback from instructional tasks, peers, coaches, etc. while learning?	Yes, maybe, maybe not, no
6. Workplace Support	Does the workplace provide goals that can guide performance "this period" and "today"?	Yes, maybe, maybe not, no
	Does the workplace provide adequate tools and materials?	Yes, maybe, maybe not, no
	Is good performance clearly rewarded more than poor performance?	Yes, maybe, maybe not, no
7. Workplace Feedback	Is regular and systematic feedback provided so that graduates can easily tell how well they are performing?	Yes, maybe, maybe not, no
	Is it easy for the instructor to receive regular and systematic information about how well graduates are doing?	Yes, maybe, maybe not, no

whether training has been carefully linked to the workplace or not. Generate both types of answers and compare them.)

- What are two or three ways that having adequate guided practice during training makes it more likely that people will use what they have learned when they return to the job?
- What are two or three reasons that having high performance standards during training makes it more likely that people will use what they have learned when they return to the job?
- Give examples in which you tried to apply new learning but met with resistance from others?
- Give examples in which you knew you could and should apply what you learned, but did not?
- What are some simple and practical things that can be done to do a better job of linking training to the workplace?

The process for designing performance-based instruction provides more checks along the way to assure that linkages are formed. (See Chapter Eleven for more detail.)

An Example of a Productivity Improvement Workshop

Specification of Business Need

A consulting group linked a generic workshop on productivity improvement to the specific needs of the client. Working with people in the client organization, the consultants verified productivity improvement as a current and strategic business issue. They based the goals of the training on the business issue: each participant was to implement a performance-improvement project in his or her work area.

Specification of Performance Requirements

The consultant worked with each participant before the first session to identify potential projects. Specific opportunities for improvement and data sources to verify the opportunities were identified.

Design Phase One: Specification of Work Processes

The deliverables were the completed projects; the consulting company provided the training and the follow-up support needed to assure that the projects were completed successfully. The client organization agreed to provide opportunities for the consultant to work with each participant before, during, and after the workshop. The client organization also agreed that only people for whom a project could be identified would be participants; people without a project were to attend only when conditions changed so that a project could be identified.

Design Phase Two: Specification of Instructional Processes

A performance-based workshop was designed. Two-hour training sessions were scheduled once a week for several weeks. The workshop leader was scheduled to work, on-site, with each participant for at least one-half hour per week to collect data for problem analyses and to help implement solutions. The workshop leader also met at least twice with the participants' supervisors. The meetings were progress reports, descriptions of exemplary results, and discussions of the support the participants needed to complete their projects.

As for implementation and evaluation, several key events occurred during and between training sessions.

Guided Observation

1. Each participant worked through an exercise during which he or she identified several areas of potential improvement and did a cost-benefit analysis for at least one area.
2. The workshop leader worked through an analysis of one of the areas of focus, identifying deficiencies in support systems (e.g., tools, materials, or feedback) and deficiencies in management systems (e.g., goals, incentives, guidance, priorities, or information).
3. The workshop leader lead a discussion of the procedures used in the analysis, then led the group through another analysis.
4. The participants, working in small groups and with support from the workshop leader, completed analyses of performance-improvement projects for each participant.

Guided Practice

1. The participants worked in small groups to design solutions for each problem. Additional knowledge about productivity improvement was provided at this stage by the leader.
2. Each participant implemented solutions for one or more of the problems he or she brought to the workshop. Guidance was supplied during the workshop leader's weekly meetings and from the well-briefed supervisors.

3. The workshop leader made reports of progress and problems encountered, reporting back to participants and to top management of the client organization.

Demonstration of Mastery

Mastery was demonstrated by successful implementation of projects. Each project included evaluation of results so that it was easy for everyone involved to see how well projects were doing.

Analysis of the Example

1. Is this sort of collaborative agreement between a consulting firm and a client organization common?

Yes, but not common enough. The example is based on work done by Sheldon Stone when he was an associate at Feeney Associates; Aubrey Daniels and his colleagues at Performance Management do similar work routinely. But such collaboration is too often absent, not only between external consultant and client organization but also between HRD departments and internal clients.

2. How successful are the projects?

Nearly all participants complete a project successfully. The economic value added by all the projects completed by one group of participants typically assures that the performance-based training is an economic success. Some projects add greater value than others, of course. Some are selected more to reduce sore spots than to add economic value. From an adult-learning perspective, a project that reduces immediate pain can be more valuable to a participant than one that generates significant but "distant" economic value for the organization.

3. Do the participants really learn much?

There is no good data. Anecdotal evidence suggests that many participants complete second and third projects on their own. That should not be left to chance, however, and internal HRD staff members and line managers should continue to support projects.

4. How long should follow-up support continue?

If the training event is truly linked to current and strategic business goals and strategies, the support should continue until goals and strategies change. At first the support is needed to assure that participants receive enough and varied practice to learn the requisite knowledge, skills, and attitudes thoroughly. Even after participants are skilled in all phases of the work, management support is needed to guide selection of projects and provide any needed resources and cross-functional support.

5. How is training linked to the prior knowledge and future aspirations of the participants?

Part of the linkage occurred before the training session when the workshop leader met with each prospective participant. The trainer collected numerous ideas for improvement and obstacles to improvement. The fact that people offered the ideas showed that they had extensive prior knowledge and aspired to improve.

Trainers sometimes use the "before" meetings to work with prospective participants to set personal goals and identify specific strengths and weaknesses in prior knowledge. It is a good way to connect a training event to the a career-development process.

Additional linkages come during the instruction. The workshop design and the workshop leader's facilitation tactics are based on adult-learning principles in which the experience of participants is fully utilized. In addition, the linkages to organizational goals and strategies help to make it safe for the participants to invest energy in learning what they can from the workshop and using what they learn on the job.

6. Are linkages easy to establish beyond productivity improvement?

The linkages are not easy to establish, even for something as basic as productivity improvement. On the other hand, linkages can and have been established for many popular training topics such as time management, coaching, interpersonal communication, safety training, delegation, supervision, self-management, career development, performance appraisal, motivation, and many others. The authors know of no one who has established the before and after linkages for topics such as finance for nonfinancial managers, diversity training, or sexual harassment. Designs for performance-based training in these areas are straightforward and there is no theoretical, philosophical, or practical reason why it could not be done.

7. Is there a specific process for establishing the key linkages?

One potential procedure follows:

- *Business Need Specification*: Ask basic questions and work with others to formulate the answers as a business need specification that spells out the results being sought.
- *Performance Requirement Specification*: Ask basic questions and work with others to write a document that specifies the performance that will yield the results.

Preparation of these two specification documents develops a shared understanding of where the project is going.

- *Design Phase One*: Prepare a plan for supporting what is to be learned, being sure to include (a) the processes learners will use to generate the products or results and (b) the performance-support processes to support participants during instruction and afterward in the workplace.
- *Design Phase Two*: Design an instructional system that provides guided observation, guided practice, and demonstrations of mastery and assures that some of the observation, practice, and mastery demonstration occurs in the workplace.
- *Implement and Evaluate the Instructional System*: Implementation and evaluation occur all along the way as we check to be sure that we design what is needed and that the workplace environment supports the desired performance.

How the Linking Process Works

The process of linking training to the workplace is nothing more or less than developing instruction that enables people to produce specific products or services that are valued in the workplace. Figure 9.2 shows the major linkages required.

The seven key linkage points are:

1. The *goal* or *mission* of performance-based training is to add value to performance in the work environment. Neither the client nor the consulting company would have considered the program successful if the performance-improvement projects had not been completed successfully.

2. There are many *inputs* to performance-based training. The key inputs, for purposes of linking to the work environment, are real or realistic work tasks to be performed. That is why the instructor made sure that participants brought potential projects to the workshop.

3. The *training environment* simulates the work environment in key ways. The instructional processes simulate work processes: Participants analyze workplace problems, make plans, try out the plans between sessions, and discuss results.

4. *Outputs* are plans for performance improvement. In the case of the productivity improvement workshop, these plans were very tightly linked to the workplace—and were actually implemented.

5. As each plan was made, participants received *feedback* from other participants and from the facilitator that allowed them to make corrections and improvements prior to implementing the plans.

FIGURE 9.2. THE PERFORMANCE-BASED INSTRUCTIONAL SYSTEM: LINKAGES BETWEEN TRAINING ENVIRONMENTS AND WORK ENVIRONMENTS.

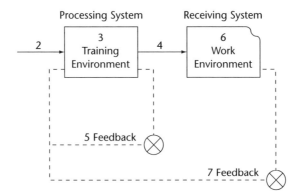

6. The *work environment*, including all the problems and obstacles and competing demands that occur in real workplaces, is the focus of performance-based training, as the arrows indicate.
7. As each step in a performance-improvement project is planned and implemented, both learners and instructors receive clear *feedback* on what works and what does not. Feedback allowed participants in the productivity improvement workshop to make adjustments and improvements during the course. Performance-based training is typically scheduled over several sessions to allow for feedback.

   The linkages are what assure that principles of adult learning and motivation and the principles of transfer of training are meaningfully applied.

Guided Observation

Guided-observation exercises occur in the work environment whenever possible. Learners are not left to wonder how the training relates to the workplace; they see the relationship from the beginning.

Guided Practice

The relevance of guided practice is assured when much of it occurs in the workplace. The instructor and other participants provide feedback to guide the practice in most performance-based training courses. Participants in the productivity-improvement workshop practiced how to learn from one another, how to help one another, and how to provide constructive feedback to one another. There is, typically, some carryover into the workplace of practical teamwork but, of course, the carryover will be both minimal and short-lived unless something is done to support it. (The only support of this sort provided in the productivity-improvement workshop was the support of the supervisor for the duration of the workshop.)

Demonstration of Mastery

The most important feedback comes from the success of the workplace applications. The productivity-improvement workshop placed great emphasis on measured performance improvements; this emphasis is typical in performance-based instruction.

Tips and Caveats

1. The folklore of training and development includes many anecdotes about major effects from single training episodes, but that does not mean that making linkages is not necessary. A common feature of the anecdotes about one-time training success is that the training event happened at just the right time in the person's life. It was well linked to the learner's past and future. Training events are but brief episodes in the lives of learners and the function of organizations. If the brief episodes are to have important and lasting effects, the training must be linked to and applied in the workplace.

2. The learning process involves making linkages to past experiences; motivation involves making linkages to aspirations and goals. Adult learners will make linkages whether or not the trainer intends it. Common unguided linkages are "We tried something like that and it didn't work!" or "Our situation is different!" or "My boss wouldn't support that!" or "That's too much trouble!"

3. Frank discussion of obstacles to applying learning frightens some instructors and some learners, but adds credibility for most adult learners. Adults have learned from experience that every silver lining has a cloud.

4. If one of the seven linkages is weak or missing, effectiveness is reduced but the omission is not usually fatal. If several linkages are missing, the instruction will not be successful in assuring that learning occurs *and* transfers to the job in ways that benefit individuals and the organization. Figure 9.3 shows seven types of linkage deficiencies and what commonly happens as a result.

FIGURE 9.3. RESULTS OF COMMON DEFICIENCIES IN INSTRUCTIONAL SYSTEMS.

Features	Common Deficiencies	Common Results
1. Goal or Mission	Lack of clarity about the performance to be improved as a result of instruction.	Different stakeholders, including learners, expect different things and work toward conflicting goals.
2. Inputs	Materials contain irrelevant material or "nice to know" or "just-in-case" material; materials fail to focus on relevant performance problems, products, or processes or standards.	Needed information is buried in unneeded material or missing entirely, making it difficult or impossible for the learners to master the knowledge or skills and acquire relevant attitudes.
3. Instructional Processes	The "how to do it here" is ignored or left to chance; learners are given too few examples of good and poor products and good and poor processes; learners are given too little practice time.	Learner energy is wasted; practice time is consumed with other activities; mastery is not defined or not efficiently achieved.
4. Outputs	Outputs of many or most instructional tasks are unclear or artificial rather than real or simulated work. Product standards for real or simulated tasks are left undefined.	Learner time and energy is wasted; learners learn how to do artificial tasks, but not real work tasks. Real or simulated tasks, if learned at all, are not mastered well enough to be performed confidently.
5. Instructional Feedback	Little feedback is provided while learning.	Learning is slow and inefficient with much wasted effort. Level of achievement is low, and there are uncorrected errors.
6. Workplace Support	Left to chance.	Learners learn that what they learn is not important to people in the workplace and what they do in the workplace is not important to the instructor.
7. Workplace Feedback	Feedback to the trained person is infrequent or conflicting. Feedback to the instructor is infrequent and unsystematic.	Trained person's performance deteriorates; instructor doesn't find out what has been successfully applied, what hasn't, and why.

Practice Exercises

Guided Observation Exercise One

Do one or more of the following:

1. Attend a training event. Interview people there, asking them about linkages to before and after. Plan to ask questions similar to these:
   - What did you do to prepare for this training?
   - Did you meet with your boss or members of your work team?
   - Did they suggest specific things you should learn?
   - Is there a specific plan to use what you learn here? What is that plan?
2. Interview people about training events they have attended in the past, asking about linkages before and after.
3. Interview people about a training event that they will attend soon, asking about before and after linkages.
4. Interview people who send others to training, asking about before and after linkages.
5. Do a role play of one of the interviews above.
6. Interview several people who are about to attend a training event, asking about before and after linkages.
7. Attend a training event. Observe the level of involvement of participants. Then determine whether there is an association between before and after linkages established beforehand and the level of involvement of people.

Guided Observation Exercise Two

1. Attend a training event. As each lesson or activity unfolds, observe the efforts of instructors to make before and after linkages. Observe the level of involvement in activities in which the instructor established multiple linkages and in activities in which few linkages were established.
2. Describe how linkages were established at each of the seven linkage points shown in Figures 9.1 and 9.2. Then describe improvements that could be made at each linkage point, using the form in Figure 9.4.

Guided Practice Exercises

Do one or more of the following:

1. Work with someone who sends others to training. Discuss before and after linkages and work with the person to establish before and after linkages. Evaluate the results.

FIGURE 9.4. WORKSHEET: EXISTING AND MISSING LINKAGES.

Linkage Point	Linkage Present	Linkage Improvement
1. Goal or Mission		
2. Inputs		
3. Instructional Processes		
4. Outputs		
5. Instructional Feedback		
6. Workplace Support		

2. Assess an existing training event regarding the current linkages. Improve linkages. Use Figure 9.4. Select a successful training event that has many of the characteristics of performance-based instruction. Improve the before and after linkages without changing the event in any significant way.

3. For the next training event you will attend, develop a plan for establishing before and after linkages for yourself. Implement the plan.

4. Design one or two action projects into your next training event. Follow the training design from the productivity-improvement workshop described at the beginning of the chapter, if you wish.

5. Establish firm before and after linkages for the next training event that you design.

Demonstration of Mastery

Think about work you do now, or might do in the future, to enhance transfer of training and/or increase your skill in doing so. Use a summary tracking chart similar to Figure 9.5 to measure your progress in establishing linkages and, in the process, improve transfer of training and obtain information about the added value of doing so.

FIGURE 9.5. DEMONSTRATIONS OF MASTERY.

Project	Goal	Start	End	Comments/Results

CHAPTER TEN

NEEDS ASSESSMENT AND PERFORMANCE-BASED INSTRUCTION

An Overview

Where Are We Going?

Needs assessment is the analysis phase. Done well, it puts the design on track so that training is part of a total project that closes a performance gap. The analysis begins when someone, perhaps a manager or a member of the HRD staff, suspects that a problem exists. It ends when it is clear that the suspected problem is not really a problem, when the problem is verified but can be solved without training, or when the problem is verified and the training component of the solution is specified.

- *Purpose*: Needs assessment is intended to assure that people receive the training they need and benefit from it.
- *Benefits*: Effective needs assessment assures that training adds value to people and to the organization without wasting resources, by minimizing costs of not training or costs of offering training that is irrelevant, unnecessary, harmful, or simply lacking in value.
- *Drawbacks*: Doing needs assessment effectively adds to the cost of training, partly from an increased cycle time. The added time is especially vexing when a last-minute training request comes in or when an unexpected and urgent performance problem occurs.

How Shall We Get There?

We will analyze an example, observing that the performance-based needs-assessment process involves seeking answers to three questions:

1. What performance gap exists?
2. What are the causes of the gap?
3. What must be done to close the gap?

Answering the questions is sometimes as simple as talking to people, listening to what they say, and preparing to take action. Performance-based needs assessment seeks to find out what workplace performance is needed but not occurring or what workplace performance occurs that should not—a mismatch between what is and what should be happening.

Performance-based needs assessment is not about surveying to find out what training people want, but about identifying performance gaps and the multiple things that must be done to close them. It is no surprise that performance gaps in real organizations typically have multiple causes. Lack of clarity about goals, competing priorities, inadequate tools, materials, feedback, or guidance are among them, as is inadequate knowledge or skill. Because the gaps have multiple causes, solutions must have multiple facets.

How Will We Know We've Arrived?

Success is when the basic questions are answered to the satisfaction of key players who, collectively, agree on the answers. It is good practice to spell out the answers in a meeting with key stakeholders, all together or one-on-one, that is documented by a report or follow-up memo of understanding, covering information provided in Figure 10.1.

When people sign off by consensus in a group meeting or by agreeing to the content of a memo of understanding, we have not only succeeded but have documented the result. Of course the agreement will sometimes be altered later, just as engineering changes occur after design specifications for a product have been agreed on.

Readers may use the self-assessment checklist that follows to assess their understanding of the needs-assessment process in performance-based instruction:

> ### Self-Assessment Checklist
> - What are some of the advantages and disadvantages of focusing on performance gaps when doing needs assessment?

FIGURE 10.1. NEEDS-ASSESSMENT QUESTIONS AND PRODUCTS.

Phase	Evaluation Questions	Evaluation Products	Comments
Business-Needs Specification (Where are we going in terms of results?)	What is the strategic or current business need for performance improvement?	Business needs agreement, i.e., a memo of understanding (or other report) summarizing the business issue, the performance gap, and measures of the gap.	Getting agreement early on the desired business results focuses the entire project and sets up Level IV evaluation, i.e., "Did we get the business result?"
Performance Requirement Specification (Where are we going in terms of performance?)	What performance products are needed to achieve the business results? What are the quality standards? How will excellent performance be supported in the workplace?	Specifications for two deliverables: 1. The products learners will be able to produce and the performance standards for them. 2. The performance support that will be available in the workplace.	Assures that any training to be done is one component, along with systems changes or performance support, of an integrated effort to reduce the performance gap.

- What are some of the disadvantages of sending out a questionnaire to assess training needs?
- What questions might be put on a questionnaire to obtain leads or ideas about important performance gaps?
- Imagine that someone asks whether diversity training is needed. What are some possible performance gaps that might justify a diversity training program?
- Imagine that an HRD manager receives a request for a course in listening skills (or writing skills or interpersonal skills or negotiating skills). What are some questions to ask to determine whether the request relates to a performance gap?
- If an HRD manager has requests for several different courses, how might he or she establish priorities among the requests and be responsive to the requests?
- Could the checklist presented in Figure 10.5 be used to evaluate the quality of any needs assessment work?
- What are some examples of situations in which people's time and money are wasted or used inefficiently due to inadequate needs assessment?
- Do I know how to build the search for performance gaps into a training course so that it occurs as part of the course?

As usual, the chapter provides several practice exercises that can be used in acquiring mastery and demonstrating it.

An Example of Performance-Based Sales Training

Several important decision makers for a retail chain believed that a sales training program was needed. Several different training programs had been used over the years, with varying degrees of perceived success.

Business Need Specification

What performance gap exists? The HRD staff member assigned to the project began by asking questions such as "What problems are being experienced?" "Are sales down in some areas where demand seems to be high?" "Are we receiving customer complaints?" "Frequent returns?" "High turnover?" "Are we planning to expand into new markets?" "Open additional stores?" Not all of the questions were answered, of course, but it became clear that there was widespread belief that a training program was needed. The analyst summarized the findings in a memo to the people interviewed, thanking them, and asking for second thoughts or corrections.

The summary concluded that several business results were being sought:

- Assurance that the sales process across departments and stores was consistent with the company image
- Improved customer satisfaction
- Reduced returned merchandise
- Reduced paperwork errors stemming from salespeople
- Timely and effective training of all new salespeople

The analyst described two major performance gaps to be corrected:

1. A gap in HRD performance: timely delivery of quality training for new salespeople
2. A gap in the quality of sales performance

Several sales quality measures would be used to track improvements in performance: consistency with the company image, reduction of paperwork errors, reductions in returned merchandise, and improvements in customer satisfaction measures.

Performance Requirement Specification

The causes and action steps for closing the gap in training delivery were identified as follows:

- The causes of the gap in timely delivery of sales training for new salespeople were straightforward. Sales training classes were run whenever enough requests came in to fill a class. The training department was evaluated on the basis of number of classes offered and number of people taking the classes. Running classes for small numbers of people made the training department look inefficient; waiting for enough people to fill a class meant that untrained salespeople were sometimes on the floor for a long time, doing the wrong things and failing to do the right things.
- The first step was to evaluate the sales training course in terms of timeliness, i.e., the time between hiring and training. The second step was for the HRD staff to learn how to design, implement, and evaluate just-in-time training. Staff would learn by doing, starting with the sales training course.

The causes and action steps for closing the gap in performance quality were identified as follows:

- There were no agreed on sales procedures or standards of sales performance within most departments, between departments in a store, or between stores. For departments that lacked specified procedures and standards, salespeople could not know what they were supposed to do and how, their managers could not give them feedback about how they were performing, and there could not be consistency or planned variation across departments and across stores. When specific departments had procedures or standards, the procedures or standards often conflicted. Similarly, there were no agreed on performance goals relevant to expected sales volume, store appearance, etc.
- Step one was to agree on what not to do. Training could establish sales procedures and set its own standards of sales performance either deliberately or de facto by whatever was taught in sales training. This had been done in the past but the procedures and standards, unsupported, had fallen by the wayside. The analyst proposed that HRD staff work with people in the departments and stores to establish an overall sales process. The process description would specify the tasks, e.g., welcoming customers, displaying merchandise, or completing sales transactions, and establish tailored standards that supported variations for unique situations. Once the process, standards, and goals were agreed on, HRD would produce a just-in-time training course to teach the process, tasks, tailored standards, and agreed upon goals.

Analysis of Sales Training Example

1. Was the proposal to develop standards accepted?

The proposal was not accepted. Having discovered the need for timely training, managers did not want to take the time to develop standards. However, the HRD manager was not deterred. She developed a plan for piloting the training, working with a few departments in a few stores: "We're developing a new sales training course and would benefit enormously from your expertise. How should salespeople present themselves to customers? If you saw a salesperson approaching a customer properly, what would that look like to you?" She also invited a few very influential department managers to serve as evaluators for the sales training course: "Would you be willing to attend the final session of one of our training classes and evaluate what we are teaching? They'll role play a few complete sales episodes and we'd like you to tell us if they do it well enough to meet your needs." Her goal was to involve more and more departments and stores until she had accomplished what the analyst had proposed about developing standards. She was not completely successful because turnover of department managers was too rapid, but the sales training was very successful.

2. Why did the analyst emphasize sales quality?

The business-needs analysis revealed many different concerns among stakeholders, too many to provide direction and too important to neglect. Grouping the majority of the concerns under the heading of sales quality gave the training program a focus that was easy to describe to stakeholders and trainees in a way that showed that their concerns were being heard. Defining the gap in terms of sales quality set up the impact evaluation for the training course, as each measure of quality could be tracked over time.

3. Why was sales volume not the emphasis?

The analyst expected a measurable impact on sales volume but wanted to credit that goal to the support provided by managers in the field. She was saying, in effect, "If you have new salespeople who can do a quality job, will you be able to work with them to increase sales revenue?" She positioned the sales increase as a goal for managers, as their motivation for providing the support needed after the training sessions.

4. How does needs assessment for performance-based instruction differ from needs assessment in general?

General needs assessment procedures look for a variety of gaps in perceived value, such as gaps in awareness of problems, issues, or opportunities or gaps between what training is available and what people believe they need. Performance-based needs assessment procedures seek a specific gap between existing performance and the performance required to achieve a current or strategic business result.

General needs assessment and performance-based needs assessment procedures can be very different, but need not be. It is good practice to validate people's perceptions against hard data, and it is good practice to be sure that any performance gap discovered and the connection between the gap and a desired business result are perceived by key stakeholders.

5. Why do both analyses?

The business-needs analysis verifies the existence and importance of a problem or opportunity. Only if a business need or opportunity exists is a performance analysis used to identify the performance needed and what must be done to support it. Knowing what must be in place to support performance enables the analyst to discover the causes of deficient performance and to specify action steps to correct the causes. The business-needs analysis provides the banner for the band wagon the training program will ride on, answering the question "Why are we doing this?" The business-needs analysis also makes it clear that HRD is only one of several riders on the band wagon.

The performance analysis answers the questions: "What must people accomplish?" "What tools and materials and feedback and incentives already exist and what must be added?" "What performance must trainees exhibit to demonstrate mastery?"

6. Is doing a business-needs analysis just common sense?

Common sense also tells us that people often will not have taken time out to reach consensus on precisely what the business need is. Different stakeholders can have different perceptions, some of which conflict. In our experience, a specific agreement often cannot be reached until after the performance analysis. Once the business analysis is done—or well under way—the special expertise of the HRD professional comes into play. The HRD professional can help to do the following:

- Focus on the specific results required to achieve the business goal
- Define the causes of performance deficiencies
- Specify the success factors that will yield the results desired

That is why we do the business-needs analysis and the performance analysis together. It is better to clarify up front than disappoint later.

How Performance-Based Needs Assessment Works

The needs-assessment process is asking questions and seeking coherent answers to them. It begins with questions about whatever triggered the training request. Of course, everyone knows that good sales training is a goal, but there is much to be gained by moving from assumptions to specifications. The questions that should be asked are straightforward, such as: "Why is better sales training needed?" "What will the world look like when performance improves?" "What are people not doing that they should?" "Are some people performing well?" "Why?" Figure 10.2 summarizes a needs assessment as it might occur in a manufacturing organization.

Some HRD professionals would not be satisfied with the needs assessment shown in Figure 10.2. However, Figure 10.3 will be more familiar to many. It

FIGURE 10.2. PERFORMANCE-BASED NEEDS ASSESSMENT (ROUND ONE).

Main Question	Project Phase	Specific Questions	Sample Answers
Where are we going?	Business-needs specification	What's the performance gap, i.e., the strategic or current business need for performance improvement?	We are losing customers due to late deliveries. Part of the problem is that about 10 percent of the time we don't deliver when promised. Another part of the problem is that because of the amount of work we have in the shop, we sometimes can't promise a delivery as quickly as our competitors can; we've lost some work and a few key customers because of that.
	Performance-requirement specification	What are the causes of the gap? What must be done to close it, i.e., what performance products are needed? What standards? What performance support?	Production people claim salespeople promise unrealistic delivery times. Sales claims that production is too slow. They are both half right. We need sales orders that promise quick delivery *and* production schedules that allow us to keep our promised delivery dates. We have to replace finger pointing with realistic communication.

FIGURE 10.3. PERFORMANCE-BASED NEEDS ASSESSMENT (ROUND TWO).

Main Questions	Project Phase	Specific Questions	Sample Answers
Where are we going?	Business-needs specification	What is the strategic or current business need for performance improvement?	Delivery, on time, on schedule, and with a shorter time between order and delivery. We must reduce cycle time by reducing unnecessary down time, schedule changes, and rework.
	Performance-requirement specification	What performance products are needed? What standards? What performance support?	Production line X produces too many bad products and has too many delays due to poor set-ups and operator errors. Main causes include poor performance sup-port and untrained personnel; we must assure that performance standards are clear and reduce schedule changes that occur due to materials delays, breakdowns, and rush orders. Clear feedback is needed so that existing set-up people and operators can tell whether or not they are doing well and so that sales can keep informed about what we can actually deliver. Training of new set-up people and new operators must assure that they move up to speed quickly.

sets up Level III evaluation (Do they use it on the job?) and Level IV evaluation (Does using it have the desired results?) and shows the HRD professional what to design for. The analyses in Figures 10.2 and 10.3 enable the HRD professional to work backward from the results to identify just what knowledge, skills, or attitudes learners must acquire during the training. It is all part of knowing the answer to "Where are we going?" prior to expending the effort required to answer precisely "How should we get there?"

The next part of the performance analysis for the project illustrated in Figures 10.2 and 10.3 would be to clarify performance standards, to identify the most frequent delays and errors, and to identify which delays and errors were caused by systems problems and which were caused by knowledge, skill, or attitude deficiencies such as not bothering to find out about or not agreeing with goals and standards.

In practice, the questioning process is usually not linear—asking all the business-needs analysis questions and then moving to performance analysis and on to design. Business needs and performance analysis are part of the same process, unless it is determined early that no business need exists. Figure 10.4 shows seven specific areas that are included in the analysis before it is finished.

The sample questions shown under the figure illustrate the questions asked in the sales training example in sequence. The answers to the questions enable the analyst to specify the business-needs and performance gaps clearly enough to develop a shared understanding of what the training will accomplish and what it will not accomplish. The questions and answers also yield much of the information that will be used to design performance-based training.

The information gleaned during the needs assessment does not just go into an evaluation report or memo of understanding to be forgotten. On the contrary, it is used to set up guided observation, guided practice, and demonstration of mastery exercises when the actual training is designed.

Guided Observation

Information about the goals and mission and about differences between good and poor performance show much of what participants will be looking for during guided observation.

Guided Practice

Information about the specific products or services generated, about the processes used, about the tools and information available, and about the guidance (instructions, feedback, and incentives) available in the workplace support the design of guided practice exercises.

Demonstration of Mastery

Information about competing demands, performance standards, etc., support the design of mastery demonstrations.

Tips and Caveats

1. Even when a verified problem can be solved without training, the HRD person should continue working with the request. It is not good customer service or good HRD practice to say "Sorry, that's not a training problem!"

FIGURE 10.4. THE TOTAL PERFORMANCE SYSTEM VIEW OF THE WORK ENVIRONMENT.

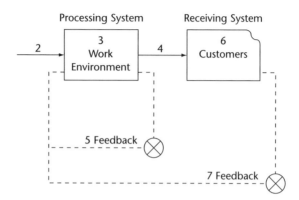

1. *Goal/Mission Questions:* What will the world look like when the (sales training) problem is solved? What current or strategic goals will be affected by better (sales training)? Why? What other initiatives are underway that would affect (sales training)? Why?

6. *Receiving System:* How will our customers, potential stockholders, or other people outside the organization see the improvement? Why? What competing forces or initiatives will be encountered? How will these affect our (sales training) initiative?

7. *External Feedback Questions:* What measures of business performance will improve? Why? What economic measures will be affected? What customer satisfaction measures will be affected? What feedback do we have that indicates how well (salespeople) are performing?

5. *Internal Feedback Questions:* What internal measures of timeliness, quality, or cost will be affected? What other internal measures is (sales training) likely to affect? What feedback do (salespeople) receive that tells them how well they are doing? How frequently and in what form do they receive it?

4. *Output Questions:* Just what products do (salespeople) generate? What services do they provide? What are our quality standards for their performance? Who, exactly, receives the products or services? Who else sees or interacts with the products or services? Do some (salespeople) do better work than others? Why?

3. *Work Environment Questions:* Who notices how well (salespeople) perform? What happens when they perform badly? What happens when they perform well? What bad things happen? What good things happen? What is their work environment like? What competing duties and activities are present? What distractions and obstacles are present? What tools and job aids do they have to work with? What are the incentives for good performance?

2. *Input Questions:* What instructions are (salespeople) given about goals and priorities? What types of materials do they work with? What are the (salespeople's) customers like? How heavy is the workload? Are there peaks and valleys?

2. More often than not, the initial training request is altered significantly as a result of the analysis. If the person requesting the training has not already thought through the issues, the analysis guides the thinking, sometimes verifying the initial hunch, always setting it in a realistic context, and sometimes changing it entirely.

3. If a topic turns out to relate to a significant business need, training will almost always be needed to close the performance gap; on the other hand, training will almost never be the only intervention needed to close the gap.

4. When a verified problem has a significant training component, the HRD professional should work with those who have responsibility for implementing other parts of the solution. Not only should the training dovetail properly with the other components, but the HRD professional should be available to coach and provide informal OJT to the people involved. For example, one component is often a change in performance standards or in supervisory feedback. This is so frequent that the wise HRD person has materials available for people to use as models or job aids.

5. Experienced analysts plan their questions carefully but are quite comfortable deviating from the plan as they obtain more information.

6. Gilbert's (1996) Behavioral Engineering Model is an excellent one to use to identify whether workplace conditions would support the trained performance or whether the performance-support systems should be improved. A variation of Gilbert's model is shown in Figure 10.5. If performance is deficient, the causes can be found by examining the workplace in terms of the variables in the six cells. The causes will relate to at least one and usually more than one of the cells.

7. One of the hardest things to do in performance-based instruction is to obtain agreement on performance standards. Almost everyone knows that performance standards have sometimes been used as a basis for berating or intimidating workers. We have all experienced it in school under the banner of "high academic standards." People resist what they have reason to fear, but we need not let that stop us. The tactic used by the sales trainer works quite well. Just pilot test and involve people in evaluating the performance standards until it is clear that the standards are used to develop and reward rather than intimidate and punish.

Practice Exercises

Guided Observation Exercise One

1. Interview a former or prospective client.
2. Describe the training design from Chapter Nine, especially the action projects and before and after links.

FIGURE 10.5. CAUSES OF PERFORMANCE DEFICIENCIES.

Causes Related to System	*Feedforward/feedback deficiencies:* Are there clear guidelines, policies, and subgoals supporting goals, priorities, and incentives? Is feedback timely, frequent, and accurate?	*Tools and materials deficiencies:* Are the tools, machines, technologies, and materials consistently adequate? Are they properly maintained?	*Goal and incentive deficiencies:* Are there relevant, specific, and generally accepted organizational goals? Are there supporting incentives? Do immediate consequences support desired performances?
Causes Related to Person	*KSA deficiencies:* Does performer (1) know the goals and incentives? (2) know how to interpret performance data? (3) believe the organization is supportive? (4) know how to do the tasks needed?	*Ability deficiencies:* Is the performer (1) healthy and physically able to do the work? (2) free of handicaps not compensated for by special tools or equipment?	*Motive and value deficiencies:* Could the person perform well given strong incentives? Does the performer value available incentives? Do performer goals support organization goals? Is fear motivation prevalent?

3. Ask if the client would share expertise on advantages of and obstacles to doing such training in his or her workplace.

Guided Observation Exercise Two

1. Talk with a former or prospective client about what he or she believes are good standards for training. Share the following four criteria (patterned after standards developed by the Joint Committee on Standards for Educational Evaluation). Good training should:
   - Serve useful purposes
   - Convey accurate content
   - Facilitate learning
   - Use resources effectively and efficiently
2. After discussing the four criteria, say "I'd like to talk with you about how people can assure that training serves useful purposes. Hearing your ideas would help me. Would you be willing to take a few minutes more?"
3. If the person agrees, say "To assure that training is useful, I think we have to do some work on the front end." Then show and discuss the criteria shown in Figure 10.6 on the following page. After a needs assessment for performance-

FIGURE 10.6. CRITERIA FOR NEEDS ASSESSMENT FOR PERFORMANCE-BASED INSTRUCTION.

A good needs assessment assures that the project will add value to the individuals being trained and, thereby, add value to the organization. The project should:

Match Organizational Needs/Opportunities!

1. Is the organizational need or opportunity specified?
2. Is the need documented with performance data relevant to one or more units within the organization?
3. Is the need documented with performance data relevant to performance of critical work?
4. Is the need documented with financial data?

Emphasize Economic Potential!

1. Have costs of not training been estimated?
2. Are the probable costs of not training large when cumulated over the next one to three years?
3. Has the potential value of performance improvement been estimated?
4. Is the potential value of improvement a substantial figure when cumulated over the next three to five years?

Consider Stakeholder Perceptions of Needs and Wants!

1. Have stakeholders at all levels been identified?
2. Is the need perceived by most managers of affected units?
3. Is the need perceived by most of the people who would receive the instruction?
4. Has stakeholder commitment been obtained from the key players?

Specify Performance Deficits!

1. Have specific performance deficits been identified for people who would receive the instruction?
2. Have deficits in specific accomplishments or work outputs been identified?
3. Have specific knowledge, skill, and attitude deficits relevant to the work outputs been identified for the people who would receive the instruction?
4. Are the probable costs of training less than the probable costs of not training?

Specify System Deficits!

1. Are tools and materials adequate?
2. Are adequate feedback systems in place?
3. Are adequate rewards or incentives in place?
4. Have goals and standards been communicated and accepted?
5. If there are inadequacies in the four areas above, are they being corrected?

based instruction is completed, you should be able to answer "Yes" to most of the questions.

Guided Observation Exercise Three

1. Before you do exercise one or two above, role play them with a colleague.
2. Do the role plays soon, even if it will be a while before you schedule the actual interviews.

Guided Practice Exercise One

1. Develop a brief business-needs analysis for existing training: What performance gap exists? What business result is being sought? What is happening that should not? What is not happening that should?
2. Show a rough draft to a client and listen to his or her reactions.

Guided Practice Exercise Two

1. Develop a brief business-needs analysis for training that has been requested. What business result is being sought? What is happening that should not? What is not happening that should?
2. Discuss it with the client and obtain approval.

Guided Practice Exercise Three

1. Do a performance analysis for an existing or proposed training course. Begin with a business-needs analysis and list the three major tasks people will perform after the training. (Use Figure 10.7 as a worksheet, if desired.)
2. Show the client the task list and ask questions about it: "Do you want people to be able to do this?" "If they can do this, is there something more you want?"
3. Revise as needed, until the client is satisfied.

Guided Practice Exercise Four

1. After establishing a business need and identifying the key performance tasks that should be performed, interview key people to discover some of the causes of performance deficiencies. Base your interviews on questions in Figure 10.5.
2. After identifying possible causes, meet with the client to discuss how the causes will be dealt with. Say something like "I need your help. By doing the analysis I learned that people on the job encounter these problems. Do you think

FIGURE 10.7. PERFORMANCE ANALYSIS WORKSHEET.

Task Name	Activity	Product/Result

new trainees would be able to cope with such problems or should we try to do something about them?"

3. Negotiate the deliverables. Specify what you will deliver and what the client will deliver.
4. Confirm the agreement with a document that summarizes the shared understanding of:
   - The business purposes
   - The performance gaps
   - The products or services trainees will produce by the end of training
   - The time, quality, and cost standards for the products or services
   - The things that will be done in the workplace to support performance

Guided Practice Exercise Five

1. Do another business-needs analysis and performance analysis.
2. Use the questions in Figures 10.4 and 10.5.
3. Negotiate agreements and document them using any format that you and the client are comfortable with, being sure to cover all of the following:
   - The business purposes
   - The performance gaps
   - The products or services trainees will produce by the end of training

- The time, quality, and cost standards for the products or services
- The things that will be done in the workplace to support performance

Demonstration of Mastery

Gaining mastery of performance-based needs assessment requires practice. Gaining complete confidence and ability in performance-based needs assessment is a never-ending task. Incorporate what you learned in the guided observation and guided practice exercises above in the next training projects you do. Design tailored analysis questions and agreement documentation formats that fit your environment. Continue until it becomes routine. Chapters Eleven and Twelve contain information and worksheets that will help.

CHAPTER ELEVEN

A STRUCTURED-DESIGN APPROACH FOR PERFORMANCE-BASED INSTRUCTION

An Overview

Where Are We Going?

The focus of this chapter is on how to use performance-based instruction for the design of complex projects.

- *Purpose*: A structured approach is used to develop performance-based instruction so that the parts of the training fit together, link to the workplace, and are consistent with principles of adult learning and human performance.
- *Benefits*: The approach allows designers to minimize cycle time and unwanted variability in quality of instruction. It supports coordination of effort among several members of the development team. The approach incorporates evaluation throughout the design process, involving stakeholders and assuring that unpleasant surprises are minimized.
- *Drawbacks*: The approach serves as a guide for developing instruction and may be inhibiting to those who use intuitive approaches. It can feel too unstructured or too tightly structured to people who are comfortable with other ways of developing instruction.

How Shall We Get There?

We will use sample worksheets to guide us through business-needs specification, performance-requirement specification, specification of training and support system deliverables, design of instruction, evaluation, and development. The worksheets contain more than fifty analysis questions, which is too many to remember, and the answers can be complicated. Novices and experts alike run the risk of becoming bogged down in details, so the worksheets have been built around a simple logic inspired by Mager's three questions (Mager, 1997): "Where are we going?" "How shall we get there?" "How will we know we've arrived?"

The worksheets are set up so that they can be used by people with little instructional-design experience and so that members of a design team can work on different parts of a design and still have the parts fit together.

Experts can use the worksheets as a tool to assure completeness and to be certain that the parts fit together. When the parts fit together, the design process is on track. Less-expert designers learn to use the worksheets by going through the familiar processes of guided observation and practice and demonstration of mastery.

- *Guided Observation*: The analysis involves both interviews and direct observation of performance. The worksheets guide the user toward important variables influencing adult learning and performance.
- *Guided Practice*: The worksheets are useful guides for doing analyses and designs. The evaluation components generate feedback to further guide practice in learning and using the approach.
- *Demonstration of Mastery*: Evaluating first efforts typically shows that the partnership between the designer and the client, guided by the worksheets, is a success. Evaluating several efforts typically shows increased efficiency and quality.

How Will We Know We've Arrived?

One can assess arrival along the way as well as at the destination because each step in the process involves asking and answering specific questions. We "arrive" each time a question is answered, as can be seen in Figure 11.1.

When we have several answers it sometimes feels overwhelming. The worksheets help us capture the information, but we must organize it into documents that are useful for managing the project or for using as instructional material. As each document is generated and approved by members of the design team or by stakeholders, we have taken another step toward a successful project.

Practice exercises at the end of the chapter can be used to assure that we learn the many skills involved in using the structured-design approach.

FIGURE 11.1. STRUCTURED-DESIGN PROCESS OVERVIEW.

Worksheet	Products Based on Worksheet Answers
1. Business-Needs Specification: Where are we going?	Memo of understanding regarding the strategic or current business issue and the perceived gap in performance.
2. Performance-Requirement Specification: Where are we going, exactly?	Specification of deliverables: learners who can produce specific products to specific standards and performance support in the workplace.
3. Design Phase One, Specification of Work Processes: How shall we get there?	Specification of processes trainees will master; of performance support that will be provided during instruction.
4. Design Phase Two, Specification of Instructional Processes: Specifically, how shall we get there?	Specification of overall structure; specification of structure of units.
5. Implementation and Evaluation	Verification of need, cause analysis, design evaluation, pilot implementation, full implementation.

Readers are invited to use the self-assessment checklist below to check their understanding of the approach:

Self-Assessment Checklist

Do I understand:

- How answers to "Where are we going?" can be put together into a project proposal or memo of understanding?
- Why it is worthwhile to generate a memo of understanding to clarify and obtain support for the direction and importance of a project?
- Why generating a memo of understanding can be a critical step for politically sensitive projects?
- Why sharing some of the information in the memo of understanding would help adult learners?
- Why we must be clear about "Where we are going?" before spending a lot of time and energy on "How shall we get there?"
- That showing some of "How shall we get there?" helps people understand or decide "Where we are going?"

- Why obtaining agreement about the material that goes on the worksheets is a good idea before spending a lot of money developing a training program?
- How the material that goes on the worksheets can be used effectively to guide development of the actual instructional material?
- Different ways a design team could be used, e.g., by having one member of the team design a unit dealing with one product people will have to produce on the job and having another team member design a unit dealing with another product?
- How to use a systematic design approach to demonstrate the ability to take a professional and orderly approach to complex or politically sensitive projects?
- That worksheet phases 1 through 4 are set up in a "logical sequence?"
- That phase 5 occurs along with phases 1 through 4?
- That real-world projects never occur in the "logical sequence" we have in mind at the beginning?
- That experts are more flexible and efficient in altering the sequence than beginners?

An Example of Time Management for Contract Administrators

The best way to see how the structured-design approach works is to examine a set of completed worksheets. The example is realistic rather than ideal, designed for a training program that is a stopgap effort related to a problem that will not be fixed until some organizational and systems changes are made. By reading the questions on the worksheets and the "answers" the designer gave, the reader can see the tension between what was needed and what was possible under the circumstances.

The designer guessed at some of the answers and discussed the real issues involved with the stakeholders. The completed worksheets should be read prior to reading the analysis.

Developing Performance-Based Instruction

Where Are We Going?

Business-Needs Specification ⟶ Performance Gaps and Potential Value

Topic

What strategic issues, current business problems, or desired results are or should be driving the project?

The twelve-person contract administration department for a high-tech company working on multiple government contracts has been restructured recently because too many contract-administration errors were occurring.

One contract administrator (CA) was assigned to a new role with added responsibilities; another left the company. There are now only ten CAs, counting the department director. No new CAs will be hired.

Context

What is the work setting in which people do the work? What products or services or measurable results are desired? What aspects of the work setting, products, constraints, and desired results are most relevant to the project?

Contract administrators monitor performance, complete necessary paperwork, and report contract status both internally and externally. They are held accountable for "keeping us out of trouble with the feds." They have been told that more work must be done in less time. Computerization of some processes which will reduce the work load is expected to occur within three years.

The CAs are salaried and expected to work as many hours as it takes to do the job. They have been told that training in time management will help them handle the increased work load and reduce errors.

Potential Benefits

What are the benefits of the project? What current business issue or strategic initiative would be supported by improved performance? What would be the long-term benefits to learners, the organization, or to society? What would be the short-term benefits? Short-term costs?

The last time the department was understaffed, morale plummeted as long hours interfered with family commitments; delays, errors, and finger pointing became the norm. It would benefit everyone if this could be avoided. Also, if the

CAs improve their productivity through improved time management, they can show those reporting to them how to get more done with less rush and confusion. Another positive benefit is that contracts will be better administered, reducing risk of lost contracts and improving the chances of further business.

Potential for Maintenance

If the performance objectives are achieved, how will the organization or society support the desired performance? What natural consequences, reward systems, social support systems, or control systems support performance? Do such support systems exist now? Do they work effectively? What must be done to assure that they work effectively in the future?

Contract Administrators are likely to continue using time-management skills as a matter of self-preservation, their only alternative, other than leaving their jobs. (Their replacements would also need the skills.) The director has pledged support for the time-management program and will attend the session and practice the skills. In addition, he has agreed to work with the workshop leader after the training session to reinforce the skills. He is willing to consider performance bonuses and added compensation for improved productivity, but is not sure that the compensation people will go along with it.

Performance Requirement Specifications

Performance Products, Standards, and Support

What do current experts/master performers produce? What permanent products or service results do they generate? Which of the products and results will learners produce when they finish the training?

The CAs produce numerous reports and documents and dash madly about helping fight fires and renegotiate contracts if necessary. During the training, CAs will identify the key reports and simplify them so that they can be done more efficiently while being more timely and more useful.

Performance Quality Standards

Products: What are the differences between good and not-so-good products/results? How do master performers or supervisors evaluate quality? How will the learners, instructors, or others determine the adequacy of the learners' outputs? What performance standards or criteria of merit or worth will be used? Processes: Will learners have the same time constraints and other standards that expert performers face?

Good products are reports that are filed on time and without errors; bad products are late, unfiled, or erroneous reports. Good administration is assuring that everyone has needed information about project status; bad administration is failure to inform in a timely manner or allowing people to ignore information received. Formal performance standards do not exist; CAs acquire a reputation either for creating or for cutting through red tape and for being on top of details or letting things get out of control. Performance standards are becoming more stringent, everyone agrees, but no one knows exactly what they are. The learners *are* expert performers, but they must become better.

Workplace Performance Support

How will performance be supported in the workplace? What tools, reference materials, job aids, guidance, feedback, incentives, goals, and standards are available to expert performers? How is good performance rewarded? How is poor performance corrected? How are competing influences managed? Will performance support be improved for newly trained people?

New systems are needed but they will not be available in the near future. CAs have stacks of regulations that they are supposed to know or refer to and a continuous stream of updates to regulations. They receive feedback every time something major goes wrong, but little positive feedback. If they turn in erroneous information, it must be corrected.

How Shall We Get There?

Design Phase One:

Work Processes and Instructional Support

Major Subproducts/Processes

What are the major subproducts? In what sequence are they produced? Draw a flow chart or show the subproducts in some other useful way. For any process that has more than five phases, also draw a three-phase summary flow chart showing beginning, middle, and end.

Most of the work is rather chaotic. A former CA did a study showing that it would be much less chaotic with better computerization, but that is on hold. The stopgap is time-management training.

The training designer has decided that there will be several specific products for the training: Participants will:

- Develop work objectives
- Identify tasks to be delegated—and delegate them
- Develop priorities for their activities
- Use some form of daily to-do list

Performance Support During Instruction

How will conditions of performance be simulated and supplemented during instruction? What job aids or other tools will be given to learners when they demonstrate mastery? What additional tools, guidelines, etc., will be available during guided practice? Will these differ from those available in the normal workplace environment?

Several job aids will be used, e.g., an activity log, a time-management survey, and a delegation form. In addition, the goals, priority lists, and to-do lists are performance support. Indeed, time-management techniques constitute performance support.

Design Phase Two: Instructional Processes

Overall Structure and Unit Structure

Use this worksheet to specify the structure for the entire instructional event; then use additional copies to specify the structure for each unit.

Getting Learners Involved

This section (overview, welcoming, icebreaking, guided observation) should present specific actual or simulated situations that expert performers and/or novice performers encounter. Learners should be involved in interpreting the situations and the value of dealing with them.

The problems—and using time-management training as a stopgap solution—have been discussed in several staff meetings. A letter from the division chief will invite the CAs to attend the half-day training at a nearby hotel beginning with breakfast and ending after a catered lunch. Five people will attend one day, the other five two days later. The letter will include a time management survey to be filled out prior to the training and an activity tracking log to use as a one-week baseline prior to the training. The department director will attend the working lunch period both days.

The objectives of the training will be reviewed at breakfast; people will brainstorm "time saving ideas"; and the session will begin with an analysis of the survey and the activity tracking logs.

Pointing Them in the Right Direction

This section would include showing them, modeling, domain/demonstration, debriefing of guided observation, and set up for guided practice. It should connect to the overview situations, showing how to interpret them using the concepts and principles learned. Examples of good and not-so-good products and processes should be included.

Department priorities and objectives will be discussed and not more than three will be selected. Individuals will then use the departmental information, plus the analysis of the survey and the activity log to develop personal performance goals.

Helping Them Do It

This component should provide frequent and specific feedback during learning, i.e., information about performance plus coaching for improvement. It involves hands-on work with specific situations.

Using the time-saving ideas from the brainstorming session, plus some additional ideas in the form of job aids, the CAs will work in pairs to identify time savers and time-management techniques to use to achieve personal performance goals. CAs will develop personal to-do lists for the next several days, listing only top priority items and leaving room for some low priority and emergency items later.

Helping Them See What Was Done

This step involves feedback, debriefing, testing, and demonstrating mastery for each product or set of products, allowing learners to experience improved performance.

CAs will share and discuss the individual goals, to-do lists, etc. As they listen to one another's plans, each CA will be instructed to find at least one idea that he or she can incorporate into his or her own plan and offer congratulations and suggestions for improvement to their colleagues.

Getting Them Out of It

This component should include specific action planning, fluency building, performance support, and follow-up. It should connect to and use the performance support that will be available in the workplace.

CAs will implement their plans, discussing progress at weekly staff meetings. In addition, during the following two weeks, each CA will meet for thirty minutes with the trainer to receive additional help.

How Will We Know We've Arrived?

Implementation/Evaluation

Business Need/Opportunity Assessment

What data or well-informed guesses are there about current and desired levels of performance? About the economic costs of any discrepancy? About the potential value of reducing the gap? Have at least three key stakeholders been identified? Have they formally signed off on the need/value?

If not, have they received a memo of understanding or other documentation containing estimates of the value of closing the performance gap?

CAs, the department director, and the division chief were in agreement that the situation was critical. They also agreed that, although the time-management training was a stopgap measure, the skills would be useful to people.

Design Evaluation

Does the instruction follow the sequence shown in Design Phase Two? Do the mastery demonstrations simulate actual conditions of performance? Are matching rules followed? Is more time allocated to guided practice than to providing information? Is there frequent feedback during guided practice? Are multiple and carefully selected good and not-so-good examples used to present all key concepts and standards? Has "nice-to-know" been set aside? Is memory load held under five items?

The adult-learning sequence is followed, from involvement to follow-up. The mastery demonstrations (setting objectives and priorities and making to-do lists, etc.) are part of the performance desired. CAs may have been letting the job run them rather than managing the job, so the planning during training, the follow-up staff meetings, and individual meetings are intended to enable CAs to gain control. Nearly all the time is engaged in job-relevant work. Most of the input is in the form of job aids and instruction in how to use them. By working in pairs and then sharing and critiquing their ideas, CAs receive many examples of how time-management techniques can be used; they will, quite naturally, try out some ideas that will not work.

Clinical Evaluation/Formative Evaluation

What material will be tried, with whom, when, how, where? What evaluation questions will be asked about need, design, implementation, liking, learning, and on-the-job use of what is learned? What data are needed? How will the data be used to improve the instructional system?

No clinical evaluation will be done. The training will go directly from the drawing board into action.

Field Evaluation/Summative Evaluation

What material will be tried, with whom, when, how, where? What evaluation questions will be asked about liking, learning, using, and the impact on business results? About performance support? What data are needed to answer the evaluation questions? How will the data be analyzed and interpreted? How will they be reported?

Field evaluation will occur in the weekly staff meetings. The major evaluation questions are: Are we keeping up with the work? What time savers could be shared? What time wasters exist? Is time being used with priority tasks? What has been accomplished through delegation? Can the time-management data be used to justify the costs of system improvements?

Analysis of the Example

1. Why did the designer choose this project?
The problem was an important one for the company and for the people involved. The designer, one of the CAs taking a graduate-level course, believed that training would not solve the problem but that it could help the CAs and the company.

2. Is this an example of converting non-performance-based instruction into performance-based instruction?
Someone had determined that the CAs needed a course in time management. The CA/designer, an extremely well-organized person, did not think time management, per se, was required, but she was able to follow orders and also design a training course that would help CAs.

3. Why didn't the answers given match the questions in the worksheet very well?
First, the questions in the worksheets are guidelines to show what information is needed, so it is possible to obtain enough information without answering every single question; second, the information needed is not always available, so an analyst must press on with "roughly right" information and perhaps find more information later. That's risky, but real judgment calls are necessary. Novices make more errors than experts, which is why it is wise to have an experienced analyst or manager without a stake in the outcome to discuss issues with. The worksheets are helpful in that the questions can be shown to the client so that the client can help make the judgments.

4. Does the structured-design approach work in most settings?
The issues raised in the worksheets are important for adult learning in general and performance-based instruction in particular. The questions do not always seem to fit. For example, the questions about CAs' products and performance standards seem to have very little to do with training in time management, but if you start from the set "We're going to do what we can to help the CAs perform better, given the constraints that exist," then the questions are quite relevant. Effectively implementing a partial solution under these circumstances is better than doing nothing. However, if people do not know something is a stopgap measure and think it will solve the problem, implementing partial solutions can be quite harmful.

5. What do you do when the business analysis or performance analysis shows that training will not help?

There are several options, all of which have been used successfully at one time or another:

- Use the analysis to show what really should be done.
- Abort the project.
- Go ahead to show that at least you tried.
- Go ahead but hold the cost down.

6. It seems that some of the questions on the Implementation/Evaluation Worksheet should have been asked earlier. Why wait?

The questions should be answered as early as possible. The structured-design approach is not intended to be linear. One is implementing—or thinking about how to implement—and should be evaluating all along.

7. Why is it called a structured-design approach?

The approach is structured to support both creativity and manageability. Design, by its nature, is somewhat creative; creativity, by its nature, is somewhat structured. We attempted to develop a process that could be used by either a design team or by an individual. It is structured so that one member of a design team can focus on business issues and figure out the value added and the risks, another member can focus on workplace feedback and performance support, another can focus on product standards, another on processes, six different people can work on six different instructional units, and the whole thing will fit together. It works reasonably well.

How the Structured-Design Approach Works

The highlights of the process are specified in the five worksheets. Each yields specific design results: Specifications of a business need, a performance gap, causes of the gap, training deliverables, and training structure, as well as verification and documentation. The process is shown in Figure 11.2.

Design Phase Two specifies the overall structure of a training event *and* each unit of instruction. The structure of the whole and of each part is determined by the nature of the learning process. The design issue is "How to start where the adult learner is, make it safe to move forward, and lead the learner efficiently to mastery of something that is useful in the learner's day-to-day work."

Whole books have been written that do not quite answer that question. The gist is captured in the fourth page of the structured-design worksheets. The struc-

FIGURE 11.2. STRUCTURED DESIGN LOGIC.

Main Questions	Project Phase	Specific Questions	Sample Answers
Where are we going?	Business-Needs Specification	What is the strategic or current business need for performance improvement?	Better contract administration to avoid major difficulties with our customers.
	Performance-Requirement Specification	What performance products are needed? What standards? What performance support?	Prompt paperwork that documents progress and keeps us in compliance with government regulations. Timeliness and good communication are essential. Performance support is weak.
How shall we get there?	Design Phase One: Specification of Work Processes	What processes can people use to produce the products? How will we guide practice?	The new software will help, but until then we'll have the CAs do better time management; at least that'll clear out some of the problems the CAs cause by being inefficient.
	Design Phase Two: Specification of Instructional Processes	Does the overall design link learners and workplace? Does each unit?	The prework and involvement of key managers will help as will the activity tracking. The time-saving ideas will be realistic because the CAs generate them.
How will we know we've arrived?	Implementation and Evaluation	Are analysis and design done properly? Do the design and implementation reflect principles of adult learning and performance?	We're being honest here. People know we aren't pretending this training will solve all the problems. What we do is realistic and will be applied immediately.

ture or "instructional flow" must be consistent throughout the instruction and from lesson to lesson so that the learner knows what to do and can devote full attention to learning.

Tips and Caveats

1. The structured-design process yields design documents but does not provide guidance for producing the instructional units, setting up training events, etc.

Just doing what the documents say should be done requires considerable skill in project management, scripting materials, etc.

2. A frequent stumbling block is the lack of performance standards in the workplace. The best tactic is to set standards of excellence based on the performance of the people who perform the best most of the time.

3. Instructional designers frequently encounter constraints. Other designers encounter similar situations: Designers of lighting fixtures discover that the architect, the builder, and the customer do not offer all the support necessary to have excellent lighting by lighting designer standards. Each instructional designer must decide on a case-by-case basis whether something compromises his or her professional integrity or whether it serves the customer well.

4. There are no general standards of mastery for what is entered on the worksheets. They are intended to be useful for either novices or experts. Each designer must develop a set of personal standards for design. (Chapter Twelve on evaluation of performance-based instruction provides a set of criteria.)

Practice Exercises

Guided Observation

1. Do one or more of the following; use the structured-design worksheets to:
   - Take another look at a training event you have designed in the past
   - Take another look at some of the work you have done in other chapters of this book
   - Do an imaginary "design" of a training event that you are familiar with

Guided Practice Exercise One

Review the sample worksheets regarding the time-management project. Make a rough draft of a one-page memo of understanding addressed to D. Bigboss that succinctly describes the strategic business issue, the current performance gap, the products learners will produce during and after the training, and the performance support that will be available to them after training.

Guided Practice Exercise Two

Use the worksheets as if you were reconstructing the analysis and design of a training course or program with which you are familiar. Based on the analysis, draft a one-page memo of understanding addressed to W. E. Makebetter that describes your recommendations for improving the training.

Guided Practice Exercise Three and Beyond

Use the worksheets to do analysis and design work. Track your progress on the form below. Enter at least one project on your professional-development plan from Chapter Four.

Demonstration of Mastery

One clue that indicates increasing mastery of the worksheets is the speed and confidence with which you are able to use them. Most people start to be comfortable about the third time. After that, the worksheets feel like a help rather than a constraint.

Another clue is the feeling that "I don't really need the worksheets anymore." Unfortunately, that is probably a false clue! (The authors feel that they make more mistakes when they do not use the worksheets, so they compromise by winging it and then consolidating their notes by using the worksheets.)

Developing Performance-Based Instruction

Where Are We Going?

Business-Needs Specification ⟶ Performance Gaps and Potential Value

Topic

What strategic issues, current business problems, or desired results are or should be driving the project?

Context

What is the work setting in which people do the work? What products or services or measurable results are desired? What aspects of the work setting, products, constraints, and desired results are most relevant to the project?

Potential Benefits

What are the benefits of the project? What current business issue or strategic initiative would be supported by improved performance? What would be the long-term benefits to learners, the organization, or to society? What would be the short-term benefits? Short-term costs?

Potential for Maintenance

If the performance objectives are achieved, how will the organization or society support the desired performance? What natural consequences, reward systems, social support systems, or control systems support performance? Do such support systems exist now? Do they work effectively? What must be done to assure that they work effectively in the future?

Performance Requirement Specifications

Performance Products, Standards, and Support

What do current experts/master performers produce? What permanent products or service results do they generate? Which of the products and results will learners produce when they finish the training?

Performance Quality Standards

Products: What are the differences between good and not-so-good products/results? How do master performers or supervisors evaluate quality? How will the learners, instructors, or others determine the adequacy of the learners' outputs? What performance standards or criteria of merit or worth will be used? Processes: Will learners have the same time constraints and other standards that expert performers face?

Workplace Performance Support

How will performance be supported in the workplace? What tools, reference materials, job aids, guidance, feedback, incentives, goals, and standards are available to expert performers? How is good performance rewarded? How is poor performance corrected? How are competing influences managed? Will performance support be improved for newly trained people?

How Shall We Get There?

Design Phase One:

Work Processes and Instructional Support

Major Subproducts/Processes

What are the major subproducts? In what sequence are they produced? Draw a flow chart or show the subproducts in some other useful way. For any process that has more than five phases, also draw a three-phase summary flow chart showing beginning, middle, and end.

Performance Support During Instruction

How will conditions of performance be simulated and supplemented during instruction? What job aids or other tools will be given to learners when they demonstrate mastery? What additional tools, guidelines, etc., will be available during guided practice? Will these differ from those available in the normal workplace environment?

Design Phase Two: Instructional Processes

Overall Structure and Unit Structure

Use this worksheet to specify the structure for the entire instructional event; then use additional copies to specify the structure for each unit.

Getting Learners Involved

This section (overview, welcoming, icebreaking, guided observation) should present specific actual or simulated situations that expert performers and/or novice performers encounter. Learners should be involved in interpreting the situations and the value of dealing with them.

Pointing Them in the Right Direction

This section would include showing them, modeling, domain/demonstration, debriefing of guided observation, and set up for guided practice. It should connect to the overview situations, showing how to interpret them using the concepts and principles learned. Examples of good and not-so-good products and processes should be included.

Helping Them Do It

This component should provide frequent and specific feedback during learning, i.e., information about performance plus coaching for improvement. It involves hands-on work with specific situations.

Helping Them See What Was Done

This step involves feedback, debriefing, testing, and demonstrating mastery for each product or set of products, allowing learners to experience improved performance.

Getting Them Out of It

This component should include specific action planning, fluency building, performance support, and follow-up. It should connect to and use the performance support that will be available in the workplace.

How Will We Know We've Arrived?

Implementation/Evaluation

Business Need/Opportunity Assessment

What data or well-informed guesses are there about current and desired levels of performance? About the economic costs of any discrepancy? About the potential value of reducing the gap? Have at least three key stakeholders been identified? Have they formally signed off on the need/value? If not, have they received a memo of understanding or other documentation containing estimates of the value of closing the performance gap?

Design Evaluation

Does the instruction follow the sequence shown in Design Phase Two? Do the mastery demonstrations simulate actual conditions of performance? Are matching rules followed? Is more time allocated to guided practice than to providing information? Is there frequent feedback during guided practice? Are multiple and carefully selected good and not-so-good examples used to present all key concepts and standards? Has "nice-to-know" been set aside? Is memory load held under five items?

Clinical Evaluation/Formative Evaluation

What material will be tried, with whom, when, how, where? What evaluation questions will be asked about need, design, implementation, liking, learning, and on-the-job use of what is learned? What data are needed? How will the data be used to improve the instructional system?

Field Evaluation/Summative Evaluation

What material will be tried, with whom, when, how, where? What evaluation questions will be asked about liking, learning, using, and the impact on business results? About performance support? What data are needed to answer the evaluation questions? How will the data be analyzed and interpreted? How will they be reported?

CHAPTER TWELVE

INTEGRATING EVALUATION INTO PERFORMANCE-BASED INSTRUCTION

An Overview

Where Are We Going?

Evaluation is thoroughly integrated into performance-based instruction because evaluation is the key to designing timely, high-quality, low-cost training.

- *Purpose*: Evaluation assures quality by designing it in. Training cannot be designed effectively by experts sitting in offices. That is especially true for performance-based instruction, because it is so closely linked to rapidly changing workplaces.
- *Benefits*: Integrating evaluation into the design process enables HRD professionals to find out what customers want up front so they can better educate and serve. It prevents common errors such as instructing the wrong people in the wrong knowledge, skills, and attitudes at the wrong time and in the wrong place. It can help reduce the huge hidden cost of not training, i.e., costs associated with performance that is not improved.
- *Drawbacks*: Most clients and many HRD professionals think of evaluation as an add-on with little value after everything else is done. They are right about

the value of add-on evaluation. Doing evaluation that way can have three outcomes, all bad: (1) it can show poor results, documenting the fact that the client and HRD professional bungled; (2) it can yield little or no useful information and be an obvious waste of time and money; and (3) it can show that the project was a success and look to others like an exercise in self-aggrandizement; reports of success can, have, and will continue to stimulate political attacks in some environments.

How Shall We Get There?

An example illustrates how evaluation techniques can be used throughout analysis, design, and implementation of performance-based instruction. The example relates a complex problem in both public education and in human resource development: assuring that people learn effectively. This chapter illustrates how evaluation was used throughout course development. It contains evaluation questions and checklists that can be used to measure the adequacy of every step of an instructional-design process, allowing defects to be corrected early before they become costly or embarrassing.

Evaluation can also be used for continuous improvement of instruction that is already being delivered. It is easier to design good training or improve it if people agree on what good training is. Good training should satisfy four sets of evaluation criteria:

- *Utility*: It should serve a business purpose and be useful to the trainees.
- *Accuracy*: It should assure that the material learned is accurate and substantial rather than superficial or faddish.
- *Learnability*: It should incorporate principles of adult learning.
- *Cost-Effectiveness*: Training should assure quality through prudent use of resources, in design as well as packaging.

The chapter contains many evaluation checklists in accordance with the four criteria above. The checklists are organized around specific criteria that can be used to evaluate performance-based instruction and instruction intended for other purposes, such as to increase awareness or provide just-in-case or general knowledge.

How Will We Know We've Arrived?

Readers are invited to use the following self-assessment to check their understanding of the material in the chapter:

Self-Assessment Checklist

Can I describe how:

- Evaluation questions asked early in development of a training program help answer Mager's question: Where are we going?
- Evaluation questions help the designer answer the question: How shall we get there?
- Evaluation questions help the designer answer the question: How will we know we've arrived at each step in the process?
- Evaluation occurs in each of the major phases of the overall process of developing effective training?
- Answers to evaluation questions guide management of performance-based instruction?
- Answers to evaluation questions (especially questions in the learnability checklists) guide the development of instructional material?
- The questions imbedded in the structured-design worksheets in Chapter Eleven integrate evaluation into the entire process?
- The four evaluation criteria (utility, accuracy, learnability, and cost-effectiveness) can be used to help obtain agreement about what good training is?
- The twenty-three standards can be used or modified to help design good training?

Can I identify:

- One or two questions from each checklist that are the most important?
- Three or four evaluation questions that seem most important among the two hundred or so offered in the chapter?
- One or two places in which a little bit of evaluation might add a lot of value?

Integrating evaluation into the entire analysis, design, and implementation process enables experts to know "we've arrived" at each step along the way on an important or complex project. However, for most HRD professionals, it is likely to take a long time before integrating evaluation becomes habitual.

The wisest approach is probably a gradual one. Several guided observation and guided practice exercises are offered near the end of the chapter to provide ideas and guidance.

Example of Evaluation and Learning-to-Learn®

The Learning-to-Learn® instructional system (featured in Chapter Thirteen) exemplifies integration of evaluation into performance-based instruction. Evaluation techniques were used to answer several basic questions: "What's the need," i.e., what performance gap exists? "What's the cause," i.e., why does the gap exist? "How can the gap be closed?" "What's the program design?" "Does the instruction work?"

Business-Needs Evaluation Question: What Performance Gap Exists?

Colleges and universities in the United States faced enormous challenges after World War II. The war effort had generated new technologies, a new sense that life is short and valuable, and an enormous social demand for a better quality of life and the consumer goods that had been unavailable during the single-minded effort at national survival. Veterans returned to mainstream society very different from the youngsters who left.

Colleges and universities responded to the veterans, to a generally increased demand for a college education, and eventually to a growth in the size of the college-age population. But as more students entered colleges and universities, many of them did not succeed. A definite and serious performance gap was identified.

This performance gap still persists for many students at many colleges and universities and is passed on to employers when people fail to graduate or barely meet academic standards that some consider too low. The business need has become more acute. After years of expansion to accommodate the results of the baby boom years, the present generation yields too few bright well-prepared teenagers to fill the dorms, the classrooms, and the university coffers. Universities must downsize, attract different students, offer new services, retain more of the students who enroll, or do all the above. A consensus has not emerged about the specifics of the current and strategic issues facing colleges and universities, but the existence of a performance gap is well known and documented in enrollment trends, graduation rates, and other data.

The strategic option of graduating more of the students who enroll is attractive to many colleges and universities, as it has been for almost fifty years. This suggests that further analysis is needed to identify possible causes of successful and unsuccessful performance.

Performance Analysis Evaluation Question: What Are the Causes of the Performance Gap?

Students leave for a variety of reasons, including illness, death, inadequate financial resources, changes in career opportunities, and inadequate academic performance. Most colleges and universities have programs to deal with some of the causes: financial aid, career counseling, and health services. On the other hand, most students at most colleges and universities receive no training in how to do their work, *learning*. They are given an array of study techniques, unvalidated as to whether the right students receive it or whether they like, learn, use, or benefit from the instruction. Learner productivity is rarely, if ever, a central concern.

The developers of Learning-to-Learn® elected to focus on inadequate academic performance, the failure to earn the required or desired grade average with a reasonable expenditure of effort, a productivity problem. Productivity, output divided by input, can be measured roughly by grade averages per term and subjective estimates of amount learned, amount of time put in, and the gain to pain ratio.

Design Phase One Evaluation Question: How Can the Performance Gap Be Closed?

Learner productivity, the developers reasoned, would not solve problems of sickness, death, and inadequate financial resources, but would make it possible for students to benefit from any window of opportunity they encountered. If learners were highly productive rather than marginally productive, they might also be more highly motivated to overcome some of the other obstacles.

Training Deliverables: A major breakthrough in the development of the Learning-to-Learn® system was the specification of the training deliverables. The key questions about performance-based training deliverables are:

- What products will learners produce?
- What are the quality standards for good products?
- What processes will learners use to produce them?

What product or products do successful learners produce and what processes do they use? There are an enormous number of student products: papers, homework, tests, answers in class, registration forms, and on and on. Students use a variety of techniques for producing each product. The Learning-to-Learn® system teaches effective processes for producing many such products, as do many study-skills courses, but the breakthrough occurred when it was determined that there is one basic student product with many manifestations or forms: *answers to questions*. Completed tests accurately answer questions; term papers are well organized answers to key questions; scholarly papers are summarized answers to questions or new attempts to answer them.

Knowing the product, it is easier to identify a process. In the case of the Learning-to-Learn® system, the full process is *asking, answering, and checking answers to questions.* The logic is clear: if "good" answers are the product, part of the process must be checking answers for "goodness" and improving them if needed. Another part must be generating answers; another part must be generating questions that are worth answering. Ask, answer, check.

Specifying the training deliverables, i.e., the products and processes and students who master them, was essential. Otherwise, the training program would deliver something else. It took an enormous amount of work to figure out how to deliver them—and, through impact evaluation, establish that the deliverables, delivered, resulted in students who were able to learn more in less time, earn higher grades, graduate in higher percentages, and so on.

Performance-Support Deliverables: What is in place or what will be put in place to support excellent performance? Bowing to reality, the developers of Learning-to-Learn® decided that little could be put in place to support the process after students master it. Instead, sections were added to the performance-based instruction about how to deal with the lack of support.

Design Phase Two Evaluation Question: What Should Be the Program Design?

The Learning-to-Learn® system evolved into two parts, the first dealing directly with learning academic content and the second dealing with learning how to cope with life while doing so. As performance-based instruction, each unit enables learners to produce a specific product such as a term paper, a mock exam, a completed homework assignment, or an action plan for dealing with a problem of life. Each product can be evaluated by the learner and the Learning-to-Learn® instructor in accord with standards of timeliness, quality, and cost (time, effort, and opportunity). Most academic products are connected to real academic tasks and are also evaluated by instructors in each learner's academic courses. Life problems are connected to real life problems—paying the rent or tuition, eating decent meals and getting enough rest, or dealing with interpersonal issues—and are evaluated by the learners and significant people in their lives. Learning to produce these products is not the main focus of the Learning-to-Learn® program, but is an adjunct that enables learners to transfer the learning skills to nonacademic tasks.

Each product has a process for generating it. The processes are similar in that each is a specific implementation of basic principles of human learning. As learners learn to produce several products they discover that, because of the process similarities, they learn new processes more quickly. They also discover that they can invent new processes for new products that they must learn to produce. At that point, they are experiencing what it means to learn to learn.

Implementation Evaluation Questions: Does Implementation Verify Analysis and Design and Does the Instruction Work?

Implementation involved teaching the system to students. Pilot versions were developed and subjected to a long, arduous, and extensive developmental testing process. Initially, learners were taught to produce only a small number of products. The processes were refined over time, products were added, and instructional exercises improved.

Level I (*Did they like it?*) evaluation was straightforward. Many high-risk students required to take the course, usually not for credit, in which the Learning-to-Learn® system was taught had a long history in which they had demonstrated an ability to not learn what they did not like. Voluntary participants could stop coming if they did not like the course. It typically did not take a questionnaire to tell whether or not students liked the course; participation and attendance provided clear signals to the developers.

Level II (*Did they learn it?*) and Level III (*Did they use it in their work?*) evaluation consisted of evaluating each instructional unit by asking questions such as "Did the quality of questions they generated improve?" "Did their answer fluency improve?" and questions such as "Did student's scores on quizzes improve?" "Did the quality of their term papers improve?" Evaluations of overall effectiveness of the system were guided by summative evaluation questions (Level IV: *Did using it do any good?*) such as "Did student grade averages improve?" "Did number of credit hours completed per student per term increase?" "Did persistence to graduation increase?"

The Learning-to-Learn® system has been evaluated and shown to be effective when (1) taught by people other than the developers and (2) evaluated by external evaluators. The validation was for applications in postsecondary education institutions, including community colleges and major research universities. The developers continue to improve and refine the system. Additional validations of workplace applications are under way.

Analysis of the Example

1: Could the Learning-to-Learn® system have been developed without integrating evaluation?

Many good study techniques taught in study-skills courses simply do not work for most people most of the time. These sometimes effective techniques had to be eliminated through evaluation; those who do not evaluate continue to use techniques they believe to be effective and continue to attempt to teach students to use ineffective techniques.

2. Does integrating evaluation into design imply that we should design randomly, trying anything and relying on evaluation to sort out what works?

Well-established design guidelines should be followed, such as showing and analyzing examples of good and less good performance, modeling effective and less effective processes, and providing opportunities for guided practice. Most designers have experience-based hunches, some of which they have learned to trust and some of which they have learned not to trust. The design process is by no means random, but learning involves adding to or working with what learners already know, which varies widely from learner to learner. Finding exercises that bring out prior knowledge in constructive ways simply requires some trial and error.

3. Is it always worthwhile to invest in extensive evaluation?

Some "training" projects are done for political or ceremonial reasons and should not be developed as performance-based instruction. Even with performance-based instruction, practical constraints limit the amount of evaluation that can be done prior to the first training event and the evaluation is done as continuous improvement work and as constraints permit. Most of the Learning-to-Learn® evaluation was done that way, in settings in which "study skills" or "reading improvement" classes were being offered.

4. What is the best rationale for integrating evaluation into performance-based training?

The best rationale is quality assurance. It is exactly the same as the rationale for "designing quality in" for manufacturing.

5. Deciding not to change the instructional environment looks like a cop-out. Should the designers have attempted to do something, rather than leaving it up to the learners?

It is a cop-out at worst and the acknowledgment of a realistic constraint at best. Identifying constraints and dealing with them openly is very useful when working with adult learners in a less than ideal world. There is a place for the tactic in many courses. The HRD professional, partnering with others to identify support-system deliverables, can change some things before the learners encounter them. Students taking the Learning-to-Learn® course know the world is not perfect and appreciate realistic approaches to dealing with its imperfections.

6. Do most HRD professionals integrate evaluation into training design and development?

HRD authorities recommend it, but many have not been able to do it. Part of the reason is that practical techniques for integrating evaluation without increasing lead time have not been discovered until recently. For example, the development of the Learning-to-Learn® system occurred during the same time frame that techniques for systematic integration of evaluation were being developed. Had the techniques been available earlier, the development would have been faster.

Instructional-systems design (ISD) processes typically intend to integrate evaluation into the analysis, design, and implementation. They commonly feature an analysis/design/implementation/evaluation (ADIE) process in some form; analysis is or should be an evaluation process and design and implementation should be guided by evaluation. Brinkerhoff (1988) and Brinkerhoff and Gill (1994) provide useful information about how to do training more effectively (and, often, just as quickly) by systematically integrating evaluation.

7. Is there more information about how evaluation can be integrated into performance-based instruction?

The worksheets and checklists and questions provided in this book give considerable detail, especially the structured-design worksheets in Chapter Eleven. In addition, several checklists are included below that are a distillation of dozens of projects we, our colleagues and associates, and others have completed over the years.

How Evaluation Integrates into the Development of Performance-Based Instruction

The Process

Figure 12.1 shows how evaluation is integrated throughout development, following the structured-design process shown in Chapter Eleven. The evaluation questions in Figure 12.1 give an overview of how evaluation is integrated. Additional evaluation questions are included in the design worksheets in Chapter Eleven and in evaluation checklists presented later in this chapter.

The five phases divide a continuous flow into chunks that we can understand, manage, and talk about. The process is holistic and organic rather than atomistic and static. The phases are somewhat linear, but blend into one another. Business analysis and performance analysis blend into one another; design phase one blends with performance analysis on the one hand and design phase two on the other.

FIGURE 12.1. HOW EVALUATION IS INTEGRATED IN PERFORMANCE-BASED INSTRUCTION.

Phase	Evaluation Questions	Evaluation Products	Comments
Business-Needs Specification	What is the performance gap? What is the strategic or current business need?	A memo of understanding (or other report) summarizing the business issue, the performance gap, and measures of the gap.	Even "awareness" training should improve performance, e.g., regulatory compliance, implementation of diversity policies.
Performance-Requirement Specification	What performance products are needed to achieve the business results? What are the quality standards? How will excellent performance be supported in the workplace?	Specifications for two deliverables: (1) the products learners will be able to produce and the performance standards for them, and (2) the performance support that will be available in the workplace.	Assures that the project connects to business issues and that any training to be done is one component, along with systems changes or performance support, of an integrated effort to reduce the performance gap.
Design Phase One: Work Process Specification	What are the processes learners will use to produce the products? What performance support will be used during instruction?	Descriptions (e.g., flow charts, procedures) of how the work is done. Descriptions of guided-practice procedures.	Assures workplace relevance and sets up the impact evaluation. Assures that "what the learner brings" and "what the workplace provides" are considered.
Design Phase Two: Instructional Process Specification	Does the overall design link learners and workplace?	Description of the overall flow of the training session. Description of the flow of each unit.	Assures relevance and applicability of the learning. Pre-training preparation by learners, action plans, and follow-up support are considered.
Implementation and Evaluation	Are the analysis and design processes done properly? Is the design adequate in terms of principles of adult learning and performance?	Project overview in the form of evaluation questions and answers at each phase, needs assessment through follow-up.	Assures that stakeholders are involved and in the loop throughout. The set of evaluation questions assures that principles of adult learning are applied throughout.

All of the phases are geared toward implementation. Evaluation occurs throughout the analysis, design, implementation, and support processes.

The Products

Evaluation, as we see it, is not an activity separate from the instructional-design process. On the contrary, it can be done so that the products of evaluation actually are some of the instructional materials and provide project-management tools. Figure 12.1 provides an overview of several products of the evaluation. Figure 12.2 shows how each product contributes to learning materials and management materials.

The Standards

The authors developed several evaluation checklists to help assure that the process is capable of yielding high quality instruction. The checklists are organized around four basic criteria for training:

1. *Utility*: good training should add value to performance.
2. *Accuracy*: good training should provide accurate and relevant knowledge, skills, and attitudes.
3. *Learnability*: good training should facilitate adult learning of knowledge, skills, and attitudes.
4. *Cost-Effectiveness*: good training should make optimum use of resources.

The four basic criteria supported by twenty-three specific quality standards are shown in Figure 12.3. Those twenty-three standards are supported, in turn, by over two hundred specific evaluation questions included in the practice exercises so that they can be used in context and avoid overloading the learner. HRD professionals who adopt some or all of the quality standards can use the evaluation checklists much as they are. Different quality standards, of course, would be supported by different evaluation checklists. For example, applying the learnability criteria to instruction that is not performance-based might be very difficult; however, the evaluation questions in the figure are "learner-centered" and quite appropriate for any type of instruction.

Guided Observation

Guided observation is an evaluation process, which is one reason that it appeals to adult learners: they are constantly evaluating instruction as to relevance, applicability, practicality, enjoyment, or whatever criteria they use. Adult learners

⌨ FIGURE 12.2. HOW EVALUATION PRODUCTS ARE USED.

Phase	Evaluation Products	Use in Instructional Materials	Use in Project Management
Business-Needs-Specification (Where are we going?)	Report describing business issue, performance gap, and measures.	Used in brochures, as the basis for a video showing support by key people, etc., to show learners where we are going and why.	Getting buy-in from key stakeholders: this is where we are going and why!
Performance-Requirement Specification (Where are we going, exactly?)	Deliverables: Performance products and standards. Performance support.	Used in overviews, guided practice, and mastery demonstrations.	Avoids misunderstandings about what must be accomplished by training and what must be accomplished by management.
Design Phase One: Work-Process Specification (How shall we get there?)	Specification of performance processes and guided practice.	Used to show learners how each product is produced, then to guide practice.	Stakeholders can see that "best practices" are being taught and shows how on-the-job coaching can occur.
Design Phase Two: Instructional-Process Specification (Specifically, how shall we get there?)	Flow of total project, including training event. Flow of each training component.	Used in overviews for total event and each lesson; guides performance of learner and trainer.	Helps in coordination with management in pretraining and follow-up activities.
Implementation and Evaluation (How will we know we arrived at each step along the way? At the destination?)	Project overview in the form of evaluation questions and answers at each phase, needs assessment through follow-up.	Used to answer trainee questions about purposes, standards, support, etc.	Integrates the phases of the project and becomes the major project-management tool.

are well-practiced evaluators, although not necessarily well-trained ones. When we work with learners to identify what is good and bad about products and what is good and bad about processes, we are integrating evaluation into training. When we work with learners to develop or to understand quality standards for prod-

FIGURE 12.3. FOUR CRITERIA AND TWENTY-THREE STANDARDS FOR PERFORMANCE-BASED INSTRUCTION.

Criteria	Standards
Utility: good training adds value to performance	Matches instruction to organizational need/opportunity. Emphasizes economic potential: (1) considers stakeholder needs and wants and (2) reduces performance deficits. Reduces system deficits.
Accuracy: good training provides accurate and relevant knowledge, skills, and attitudes.	Matches content to business needs. Matches content to substantive knowledge.
Learnability: good training facilitates adult learning of knowledge, skills, and attitudes.	Matches instructional tasks to performance tasks. Uses instructional management procedures that support student performance. Matches memory load requirements to human abilities: (1) matches instructional sequences to performance sequences, involves the learner constructively, helps the learner focus on important KSA, and provides guided practice; (2) provides for demonstrations of mastery. Supports application to workplace performance.
Cost-Effectiveness: good training makes optimum use of resources.	Uses learner time effectively: (1) schedules instructional time properly, (2) accommodates individual differences, (3) uses media prudently. Uses media to support presentation of many well-chosen examples and nonexamples. Uses all tools and materials well. Uses instructors, facilitators, or performance experts cost-effectively.

ucts or for processes, we are building evaluation into instruction. When we provide or help learners to develop quality checklists as job aids, we are integrating evaluation into instruction.

Trainers, as adults, automatically evaluate their work. Trainers are well-practiced evaluators, though not necessarily well trained. For those who wish to improve their evaluation skills, we have provided evaluation tools such as checklists and lists of questions throughout this book. There are more in the practice exercises at the end of this chapter.

Guided Practice

Guided practice, too, has evaluation built into the process. Learners practice and receive feedback on what is good and bad about their performance, i.e., what is good and bad about their products and what is good and bad about their processes. Whenever a trainer provides guided practice, the trainer is integrating evaluation into instruction.

Demonstrations of Mastery

Demonstrations of mastery are evaluation exercises in which learners show how well they perform. Evaluation is thoroughly integrated into performance-based training. That is one reason that trainers who master performance-based training must, in the process, master practical evaluation techniques. That is the reason there is a chapter on evaluation in this book and it is the reason that there are numerous evaluation checklists to flesh out the major evaluation questions in Figure 12.1. The evaluation checklists support the twenty-three standards in Figure 12.3.

Tips and Caveats

1. "Let's evaluate!" is a call for resistance. Many people learned in elementary school that evaluation means painful red marks and not much benefit. "Let's find out what works and what does not!" is better and is a more honest and accurate description of the process. Always evaluate, but sometimes it is wiser to call it "total quality management for training" or "continuous improvement" or whatever sounds right and honestly describes what you are doing.
2. Verification of the need or problem or opportunity on the front end *is* a form of evaluation commonly done, and more commonly advocated. So too are design evaluation and developmental testing and Kirkpatrick's four levels of evaluation. Evaluation, from front-end through impact, is part of performance-based instruction. In fact, it is the only form of instruction in which Level IV evaluation is routine, although it is often not well enough documented to be very visible, even in performance-based instruction.
3. Much evaluation is affective. "Do I like it?" is the question. It is the evaluation learners and bystanders and managers and stakeholders and all of us use automatically. Smiles tests at the end of courses are important, primarily because they are subjective/affective. What people say about liking instruction can sink effective training and hide ineffective training. "Do people like it?" can be a make-or-break question; it is one that cannot be avoided.
4. Getting high marks on whether people like it is politically necessary in adult learning. Unfortunately, it is not always important in dealing with captive audiences such as school children, students taking required courses, institutionalized children or adults, entry-level workers when unemployment is high, and

rank-and-file people in highly bureaucratic or authoritarian organizations. People who cannot vote with their feet can be taken for granted when the measure of instruction is the number of bodies in classes.

5. People, including our customers and students, value liking, enjoying, and having a good time. Good performance-based instruction can be and should be a lot of fun. Let us not forget that enjoyment is a major evaluation criterion.

6. If learners are not having fun, there is probably not much learning going on; if learners are only having fun, there is probably not much learning going on. Having fun is a by-product of good instruction, not a substitute for it.

7. A little bit of evaluation can be better than a lot. This is almost always true when the data are collected by a questionnaire; short is much better than long.

8. A little bit of evaluation is sometimes all that is needed to make major improvements. Formative evaluation ("How can we make it better?") costs less and is worth more than summative evaluation ("How good was it?").

9. If you find it difficult to integrate evaluation into performance-based instruction, you are doing something wrong. If you think you can do performance-based instruction without evaluation, you are doing it wrong.

Practice Exercises

Guided Observation Exercise One

Do one or more of the following exercises:

- Brinkerhoff (1988) has provided another model of how evaluation can be integrated into the development of training. Figure 12.4 shows his six-stage model. The major evaluation questions link Brinkerhoff's model to performance-based instruction. Apply them to the story of the development of the Learning-to-Learn® system or to a training project you have been involved in.

- Apply the utility evaluation questions in Figure 12.5 to a training program or course with which you are familiar. For each question, try to determine whether the issue was dealt with adequately in the course or program.

- Discuss, either one-on-one or in a focus-group format, the four criteria for good training in Figure 12.3. Guide the discussion by asking: "Do you believe that good training is useful, both to the company and to the trainees?" "Do you believe that the content of good training is accurate?" "Do you believe that good training assures that trainees learn what is in it?" "Do you believe that good training should be cost-effective?"

- Discuss the twenty-three standards in Figure 12.3, offered to assure that training is good. Discuss the utility standards first. Do they make sense to you? How could they be restated to make them better? Should any be deleted? Added?

- Make notes about what the standards in Figure 12.3 and/or standards that people suggest mean to the people you talk with. Based on the discussions, develop a set of criteria and standards that make sense to people in your organization.
- Apply the standards to a training course or program that people believe is a good one and to a program or course that people believe is not as good. Do the standards describe the good one better than the bad one?

Guided Practice Exercise One

Imagine that you work for a consulting firm that designs customized training programs. Review the utility criteria in Figure 12.5. Identify ways you might use the checklist or a similar checklist during a project in which you are redesigning a training course that the client is currently offering.

FIGURE 12.4. BRINKERHOFF'S SIX-STAGE MODEL (1988).

Stages in the Training Cycle	Major Evaluation Questions
Stage 1: *Goal Setting*	What current or strategic goals are involved? What performance is needed when and by whom to achieve the results? What D_{KSA} are involved? Would HRD pay off?
Stage 2: *Program Design*	Are instructional tasks well matched to workplace tasks? Are instructional tasks focused on assuring quality of student products and processes? Are instructional management procedures well designed? Are instructional tasks well sequenced?
Stage 3: *Program Implementation*	Is the design working? What problems are cropping up? Are trainees energetically involved in making it work?
Stage 4: *Evaluating Immediate Outcomes*	What did they learn? How well did they learn it? Did they leave with good action plans?
Stage 5: *Evaluating Usage Outcomes*	Do they attempt to use what they learned? Does the workplace support their efforts?
Stage 6: *Evaluating Impact*	Does performance improve? Do key people believe that the training made a positive contribution? Is there progress relevant to the current or strategic goal?

FIGURE 12.5. UTILITY CRITERIA FOR PERFORMANCE-BASED INSTRUCTION.

Good training should add value to the individuals being trained and, thereby, add value to the organization.

Match to Organizational Needs/Opportunities!

1. Is the organizational need or opportunity specified?
2. Is the need documented with performance data relevant to one or more units within the organization?
3. Is the need documented with performance data relevant to performance of critical work?
4. Is the need documented with financial data?

Emphasize Economic Potential!

1. Have costs of not training been estimated?
2. Are the probable costs of not training large when cumulated over the next one to three years?
3. Has the potential value of performance improvement been estimated?
4. Is the potential value of improvement a substantial figure when cumulated over the next three to five years?

Consider Stakeholder Perceptions of Needs and Wants!

1. Have stakeholders at all levels been identified?
2. Is the need perceived by most managers of affected units?
3. Is the need perceived by most of the people who would receive the instruction?
4. Has stakeholder commitment been obtained from the key players?

Reduce Performance Deficits!

1. Have specific performance deficits been identified for people who would receive the instruction?
2. Have deficits in specific accomplishments or work outputs been identified?
3. Have specific knowledge, skill, and attitude deficits relevant to the work outputs been identified for the people who would receive the instruction?
4. Are the probable costs of training less than the probable costs of not training?

Reduce System Deficits!

1. Are tools and materials adequate?
2. Are adequate feedback systems in place?
3. Are adequate rewards or incentives in place?
4. Have goals and standards been communicated and accepted?
5. If there are inadequacies in the four areas above, are they being corrected?

- How might you make use of the Accuracy Checklist in Figure 12.6?
- How could you use the learnability checklists in Figures 12.7a, 12.7b, and 12.7c?
- How could you use the cost-effectiveness checklist in Figure 12.8?

 ### FIGURE 12.6. ACCURACY CRITERIA FOR PERFORMANCE-BASED INSTRUCTION.

Good training focuses on material that is substantively accurate, bridging between a learner's prior knowledge, skills, and attitudes (KSA) and the KSA needed to meet organizational objectives.

Match to learner and to business need!

1. To what extent has instruction been modeled after a best or master performer or expert (or to what extent have exemplary standards been set, if the training relates to a future need)?
2. To what extent is the instruction focused on the critical work products related to the business need?
3. To what extent has it been shown that persons who lack specific concepts, skills, or procedures perform less well (or would necessarily perform less well)?
4. To what extent is the instruction focused on the critical decisions the performer makes related to the work products?
5. To what extent are learning activities guided by a work process description (e.g., a flow chart or list of steps)?
6. To what extent is each concept, skill, or procedure to be taught used regularly in producing the work products? Can any of the work products be completed by someone who lacks one or more of the concepts, skills, or procedures?
7. To what extent are there application exercises that require the learners to use each of the concepts, skills, or procedures?

Match to substantive knowledge!

1. What is the basis for the judgment that the content is accurate? Data published in research journals? Case studies published in trade publications? Articles published in management journals? Articles published in the popular press? Common sense? A long history of use in the setting? Opinion of a designated expert? Opinion of panel of experts?
2. What are the qualifications of the persons who have reviewed content for accuracy? Are any of them unbiased experts who have no stake in the training?
3. If new concepts are to be taught, are the concepts related to currently fashionable buzzwords? If so, are the concepts well-founded in substantive knowledge beyond the buzzwords?

FIGURE 12.7A. THE LEARNABILITY CHECKLIST.

Good training facilitates adult learning of knowledge, skills, and attitudes.

Match instructional tasks to performance tasks!

1. To what extent do student products match performance products?
   - Do student products match performance products in form and quality, at least near the end of the instruction?
   - Do student products approximate performance products throughout instruction, differing only to enhance clarity or safety or economy?

2. To what extent do student processes match performance processes?
   - Do students' ways of producing the products match the experts' ways of producing them, at least near the end of the instruction?
   - Do students' ways of producing the products approximate that of the experts as closely as is feasible throughout the instruction?

3. To what extent is instruction focused on quality of student products?
   - Are numerous examples of good quality products available to learners?
   - Are numerous examples of almost good quality products used to highlight product quality characteristics/features?
   - Are the examples real or realistic (as opposed to verbal descriptions of examples)?
   - Are there numerous discussions with or among learners about what is good about the good quality products? deficient in lesser quality products?
   - Are criterion checklists used routinely to guide discussions of sample products? progress reviews or evaluations of student products? doing assigned tasks?
   - Are criterion checklists prepared in consultation with excellent performers, those who receive the performers' products, and supervisors or managers?
   - Are criterion checklists prepared by learners or checked with them to assure that they are meaningful to the learners?
   - Are product-quality guidelines and/or quality goals or standards provided to the learners or developed by the learners as part of the instruction?

4. To what extent is instruction focused on quality of processes students use to do their work?
   - Are "how to" process description lists, flow charts, or job aids given to learners?
   - Are processes modeled for learners?
   - Are good and deficient processes modeled for learners?
   - Are differences between good and deficient processes discussed?
   - Are process-criterion checklists used when showing the processes? when discussing the processes?
   - Are process-criterion checklists prepared based on observations of expert performances?
   - Are process-criterion checklists checked by learners to assure that the criteria are applicable by the learners?
   - Are process-quality guidelines and/or quality goals or standards provided to the learners or developed by learners as part of the instruction?

FIGURE 12.7B. THE LEARNABILITY CHECKLIST (CONTINUED).

Use instructional management procedures that support student performance!

1. To what extent do the instructional management procedures support quality in student products and processes?
   - Are specific quality checkpoints identified during the process of producing the product, e.g., by identifying subproducts or by monitoring key dimensions?
   - Are there specific rework procedures for all deficient work?
   - Is sufficient time allocated for rework, when needed?
   - Is there provision for monitoring processes learners use to produce the product or subproducts and for providing feedback relevant to the processes?

Match memory load requirement to human abilities!

1. To what extent do instructional tasks operate within learner memory load limits, i.e., seven plus or minus two?
   - Are all concepts related clearly to no more than three to five main concepts?
   - Are job aids used effectively to manage memory load?
   - Are reference materials used effectively to make information only occasionally used readily available?
   - Are complex tasks broken into subtasks effectively?

Match instructional sequences to performance sequences!

1. To what extent are the tasks sequenced so that the risks or dangers or costs of performance errors are minimized?

2. To what extent does the sequence in which tasks are performed in the instructional environment correspond to the sequence in which the tasks are performed in the natural environment?
   - Are completion steps introduced before initial steps?
   - Once each step has been learned, are steps practiced in the natural sequence?

3. To what extent does the overall sequence of tasks match learner needs?
   - Do the first tasks in a sequence of tasks emphasize value issues?
   - Do the second tasks in a sequence of tasks emphasize conceptual material?
   - Do the third tasks in a sequence of tasks emphasize procedures or skills?
   - Do the final tasks in a sequence of tasks emphasize integration of competent, proficient, or fluent performance?
   - Are major tasks presented before subtasks as an outline?

4. To what extent is material within each task presented in a sequence in which learners learn?
   - First, why good products of the task are valuable and why good performance of the task would benefit the learner
   - Second, what good products are (i.e., are product quality criteria and features learned before learners attempt to produce good quality products?)
   - Third, how good products are produced (i.e., are process quality criteria and features learned before complex processes are attempted and before proficiency practice begins?)
   - Fourth, how to complete the last steps in a long or complex sequence of steps
   - Fifth, how to complete intermediate and then initial steps in a long or complex sequence of steps

5. To what extent do the final tasks in a sequence of tasks serve to relate performance of the tasks to the conditions of performance in the natural environment?

FIGURE 12.7C. THE LEARNABILITY CHECKLIST (CONTINUED).

Involve the learner constructively!

1. By the conclusion of the orientation, can the learners:
   - Generate reasons for learning?
   - State how the learning will benefit them?
   - Relate the learning to specific personal values?
   - Relate the learning to personal experiences, problems, goals, or opportunities?
   - Identify the purpose of the instruction (e.g., to enable them to achieve personal goals, achieve organizational or societal goals, to solve specific problems, respond to specific opportunities, develop personal relationships or loyalties or commitments through shared enjoyment or through shared challenges)?
2. Does the lesson provide answers to key learner questions relevant to "orientation" in Table 12.1?

Help the learner focus on important KSA!

1. Is the content summarized in no more than three to five basic points or concepts?
2. Does the lesson assure that the primitive first requirements for conceptual learning are satisfied, i.e., is each basic point supported by at least two or three well-chosen examples and three or four well-chosen nonexamples?
   - Are classification rules presented or developed to support concept attainment?
   - Is an appropriate range of examples used when mastery is tested?
3. Is each point understandable, given the examples and the learner's initial state?
4. Can all the concepts in related lessons be linked readily to the three to five basic concepts?
5. Does the lesson provide answers to key learner questions relevant to "overview" in Table 12.1?

Provide guided practice!

1. Is there a smooth flow from the overview into the guided practice?
2. Does the guided practice begin with an activity that shows the knowledge, skills, or attitudes being displayed and links them to the basic concepts?
3. Does the guided practice include practice in evaluating the extent to which the knowledge, skill, or attitude is accurately portrayed or applied?

Guided Practice Exercise Two

1. Imagine that you are evaluating the design of a course or training program for "learnability."
2. Think about a course or training event that you have designed or are familiar with. Use some or all of the questions in Figures 12.7a, 12.7b, and 12.7c to guide you. Make three (and only three) recommendations for modifying the course or training. Select three modifications that would be reasonably easy

FIGURE 12.7C. THE LEARNABILITY CHECKLIST (CONTINUED).

4. Does the guided practice provide for frequent and immediate feedback early in the practice?

5. Is the practice progressive rather than simply repetitive, i.e., in the level of proficiency, fluency, complexity, or difficulty involved?

6. Do later practice activities occur under conditions quite similar to the conditions under which mastery will be demonstrated?

7. Does the lesson provide answers to key learner questions relevant to "practice" in Table 12.1?

Provide opportunities to demonstrate mastery!

1. Do learners have the opportunity to display, in an organized and coherent way, their altered repertoire (not merely through random sampling of knowledge)?

2. Does the mastery demonstration occur under conditions that approximate those in which learners will later use, apply, or be expected to remember the new learning?

3. Are there provisions for further work, if needed, to attain mastery?

4. Are people allowed/required to finish without attaining mastery?

5. Does the lesson provide answers to key learner questions relevant to "mastery" in Table 12.1?

Support applications to workplace performance!

1. Are several techniques used to assure transfer, e.g.,
   • Practice with a broad range of examples?
   • Use of realistic conditions and examples?
   • Specific transfer planning exercises?
   • Use of realistic standards of mastery and fluency?
   • Actual on-the-job coaching by trainer?
   • On-the-job coaching by a trained supervisor?

2. Does the lesson provide answers to key learner questions relevant to "transfer" in Table 12.1?

to implement, would make a substantial improvement, and would lay the groundwork for other improvements.

Guided Practice Exercise Three

1. Think about a course or training event that you have designed or are familiar with. Use some or all of the questions in Figure 12.8 to guide you. Make

FIGURE 12.8. THE COST-EFFECTIVENESS CHECKLIST.

Good training must make optimum use of resources.

Use learner time effectively!

1. How much total learner time is involved?
2. How much does learner time cost, in total?
3. How much cost would a 20 percent reduction in learner time avoid?
4. What percentage of a learner's time is consumed in logistics, e.g., moving from one location to another, waiting for materials to be handed out or for equipment or other learners to finish, waiting to communicate with the instructors? Can that time be reduced?
5. What percentage of a learner's time is used to receive information or instructions (e.g., listening to a lecture, reading, watching a video)? Can that percentage be reduced?
6. What percentage of a learner's time is used to demonstrate mastery? Is that enough time to demonstrate mastery of each major concept or skill?
7. What percentage of a learner's time is used to receive specific feedback about her or his performance? Is that enough to guide performance effectively?
8. What percentage of time receiving feedback involves two-way communication with an instructor, facilitator, or coach? Can that percent be increased?
9. What percentage of a learner's time is used in practice and integration of material? Can that percentage be increased?
10. What percentage of a learner's time is used to unload competing, interfering, or false ideas? Is that percentage approximately as large as the percentage spent on receiving and comprehending inputs?
11. What percentage of a learner's time is used to plan personal applications of the knowledge, skills, or attitudes being learned? Is that enough to allow for realistic planning?
12. What percentage of the instructional time is focused primarily on knowledge acquisition? On skill acquisition? On attitude change or development, e.g., on affective or motivational matters? Is the largest percentage on skill acquisition? Is the smallest percentage on knowledge acquisition?

Schedule instructional time well!

1. What percentage of instructional time is devoted to:
   - Motivational functions? (Why learn it?)
   - Content overviewing? (What is to be learned?)
   - Showing examples of mastery? (How is it used?)
   - Guided practice? (How am I doing?)
   - Demonstrating mastery? (How well can I do it?)
   - Enabling transfer to occur? (When, where, why, and how will I use it?)
   - Anything else? (Can that percentage be reduced?)
2. Do the percentages match your standards of how time should be used?

three (and only three) recommendations for modifying the course or training. Select three modifications that would be reasonably easy to implement, would make a substantial improvement, and would lay the groundwork for other improvements.

FIGURE 12.8. THE COST-EFFECTIVENESS CHECKLIST (CONTINUED).

Accommodate individual differences!

1. Are there specific procedures to accommodate individual differences in:
   - Rate of learning?
   - Skills of learning?
   - Prior knowledge?
   - Goals?
   - Attitudes toward learning?
   - Confidence or fear of failure?

Use media prudently!

1. To what extent are media used to present demonstrations of effective and ineffective processes or procedures or behaviors?
2. To what extent do media support the message and not become the message?
3. To what extent could instruction be improved by spending less on slickness and more on substance?

Use media to support presentation of many good examples and nonexamples!

1. What percentage of examples are verbally described (lectures/readings) only? Could other media be used to a greater extent?
2. What percentage of examples are drawn from learner experiences (lecture/discussion)?
3. What percentage of examples are presented through careful pairings of examples and nonexamples?
4. What percentage of concepts are (also) exemplified through practice under real/realistic conditions?

Use (other) tools and materials well!

1. To what extent do mastery demonstrations use real or realistically simulated equipment and conditions?
2. To what extent are there unnecessary tools and materials costs, e.g., because of using more expensive technology than what is cost-effective?
3. To what extent are tools and materials needed for realism *not* used due to false economies, oversight, or unnecessary spending elsewhere?

Use instructors, facilitators, or content/performance experts to do what they can do best, i.e., better than other media!

1. Is the largest percentage of time used in coaching?
2. Is the smallest percentage of time spent in presenting information?
3. Is enough time spent providing specific evaluations of mastery?
4. Do their demonstrations show both mastery and error correction procedures effectively?

2. If you use the same course or training event you worked with in Guided Practice Exercise Two, determine whether the two checklists and your expertise would both lead to similar recommendations or whether each checklist would lead you in a somewhat different direction.

TABLE 12.1. LEARNER QUESTIONS, LESSON FUNCTIONS, AND LEARNING DOMAIN.

	Cognitive Domain	**Psychomotor Domain**	**Affective Domain**
Orientation	What is going on here? What do you want me to learn that I don't already know? What good would it do me?	What do you want me to do? What do I do to learn? Can I do it if I try?	How will you treat me? How am I to be evaluated? Is it safe or dangerous? Why should I expend my energy on your program?
Overview	What are the key ideas, etc., that I'm to learn? How does it all relate to what I already know? How does it all fit together?	How can I use or apply ideas, etc.? How similar is it to other things I've done?	What bad things will this help me avoid? What good things will it help me achieve?
Practice	What should I be looking for? What should I be saying to myself? How do I know if I'm understanding it?	How should I do it? How should I vary my practice to get better?	How should I feel now? What's it feel like to do it well? When will I feel more confident?
Mastery	How well do I need to know it? What parts should I know best? What tools can I use?	How quickly should I be able to do it? How much effort should I put in?	What happens if I make a mistake? Will I be able to try again? Will I be embarrassed? Will outstanding work be recognized or rewarded?
Transfer	When, where, and how can I use what I've learned? How does this relate to other things I know?	How can I use this in a real situation? What do I have to do to keep using it?	What do I value that this competes with? What do I value that this helps with? How can it feel natural?

Demonstration of Mastery

Do the following exercise numerous times.

1. Prepare a business-needs specification and a performance-requirement specification that develop a shared understanding of the performance system and identify opportunities to improve performance.

2. Prepare a plan for supporting performance. Assure that the plan includes specifications of:
   - Training deliverables, i.e., what products learners will produce and what processes they will use
   - Performance-support deliverables, i.e., what people in the workplace will do to support high levels of performance
3. Design an instructional system that provides guided observation, guided practice, and demonstrations of mastery and assures that some of the observation, practice, and demonstrations of mastery occur in the workplace.
4. Implement and evaluate the instructional system, checking to be sure that the workplace environment supports the desired performance.

CHAPTER THIRTEEN

PERFORMANCE-BASED INSTRUCTION AND LEARNING-TO-LEARN®

An Overview

Where Are We Going?

Performance-based instruction illustrates "systems thinking," one of five disciplines described by Senge (1990). In addition, it can be used to develop "personal mastery," another of the disciplines. For at least thirty years, individual success has been closely associated with the ability to learn. Now, individual and organizational success depends on the ability of people in the workplace to learn new things quickly and well. Senge (1990) has taken the lead in popularizing the concept of the "learning organization." However, he does not attempt to show how to establish personal mastery.

Others have stated, in effect, that the way for individuals to achieve personal mastery is to learn how to learn. The concept of learning to learn, widely discussed in educational and training circles, is simply the notion that people can learn better ways of learning (Brethower, 1990; Carnevale et al., 1990; Derry & Murphy, 1986; Heiman, 1987, 1991; Heiman & Slomianko, 1993, 1994; Johnson & Layng, 1994; Means, Chelemer, & Knapp, 1991; Smith, 1961; Snyder, 1992; Whimbey, 1975).

In spite of all the interest and discussion, only one system for learning to learn has been validated in educational settings and in workplaces, trademarked under the name Learning-to-Learn®. The system, developed by Heiman and Slomianko and validated in 1983, is the focus of this chapter.

- *Purpose*: The purpose of Learning-to-Learn® is to increase people's ability to learn quickly in the natural environment of the typical workplace or school.
- *Benefits*: People benefit by having increased opportunities for success. Organizations benefit by avoidance of training costs and reduction in opportunity costs and costs of employee turnover. A school using Learning-to-Learn® benefits through reductions in dropouts, increased competence of graduates, and decreased costs of support programs.
- *Drawbacks*: A central part of Learning-to-Learn® is learning to ask good questions, think creatively, and evaluate proposed solutions to problems. This has an impact on supervisors or teachers, as empowering workers or students with these skills leads to sometimes painful changes as difficult questions are asked, old answers are challenged, and flaws are identified that might otherwise have gone unnoticed.

How Shall We Get There?

We will look at an example of how Learning-to-Learn® was used in one organization to help people solve workplace problems. As we will see, Learning-to-Learn® is typically taught in a group or classroom setting, using performance-based instructional techniques.

- *Guided Observation*: Specific skills for producing specific academic or workplace products are demonstrated. For example, students might learn the characteristics of a good expository paragraph. Discussions and demonstrations (showing good and bad examples) are used to enable the learners to discriminate between good and bad products and good and bad processes for generating the products.
- *Guided Practice*: Learners practice the skills with real workplace or school tasks, receiving coaching and feedback from the course instructor, from peers, and from other instructors or managers.
- *Demonstration of Mastery*: Mastery of a specific skill set is demonstrated when the academic or workplace task is completed successfully as "graded" by the teacher of a composition course or a manager who evaluates the action plan. Mastery of a skill set is also demonstrated a second or third time when it is combined with another skill set to generate more complex performances.

How Will We Know We've Arrived?

First, each reader can use several self-assessment questions embedded in the chapter. Answering the questions and discussing the material with colleagues can help assure understanding. Readers are also invited to use the following checklist to assess understanding:

Self-Assessment Checklist
Can I:

- Identify or describe some of the results of using Learning-to-Learn®?
- Identify or describe several areas in which it would be beneficial to improve my learning skills? the learning skills of others?
- Describe several products that are or should be generated during workplace learning? during academic learning?
- Describe a three-part process for generating each of those products?
- Illustrate the process by describing how several learning tasks could be performed?
- Describe how to provide guided practice for performing some of the learning tasks?
- Identify ways in which trainees could demonstrate mastery of several learning skills and tasks?
- List three or four questions to use in a guided-observation exercise, making sure that at least one question emphasizes "What?" (cognitive domain issues) "Why?" (affective domain issues) and "How?" (psychomotor domain issues)?

Second, readers can actually practice in improving their own learning skills or the learning skills of others.

Third, readers can master several learning skills and weave them into a flexible and useful personal learning style.

Colleges using Learning-to-Learn® have increased the percentages of students continuing on in school by 25–35 percent; colleges or universities using it in special programs for high-risk students find that 10–20 percent more of the high-risk students graduate than do regularly admitted students. At Boston College approximately 98 percent of students classified as high risk based upon cognitive ability scores graduate if they take the Learning-to-Learn® course. That is somewhat higher than for the typical student at Boston College (typically with much higher cognitive ability scores) and considerably higher than for other high-risk students receiving other support programming at Boston College. At Roxbury

Community College, 70–80 percent of the students taking the Learning-to-Learn® course as freshmen graduated, as compared to 40 percent for students who spent comparable time in subject matter tutoring.

At a pilot implementation in the workplace (described below), over $200,000 in cost savings resulted from work done by Learning-to-Learn® students during the time the course was in operation. In another pilot, Learning-to-Learn® students were perceived by themselves, peers, and supervisors to significantly improve workplace performance.

An Example of the Learning-to-Learn® System

The Learning-to-Learn® system was taught to several workers. Instruction occurred during work hours but off the job; the workers met one hour per week for several weeks.

Guided Observation

The first session emphasized question-asking skills. Workers were shown several examples of questions effective learners typically ask. They then reflected on their experience and generated lists of questions that were (and were not) typically asked in the workplace. Each worker also generated three questions that he or she would like answered relevant to his or her work. The group then discussed the questions: "Which were most important?" "Which could they probably find answers for?" "What would they be able to do, if they had the answers?"

Guided Practice

Each learner identified at least one question worthy of being answered and noted when, where, how, and of whom the question would be asked. At the next class session, experiences with the questions and answers were shared and discussed. Learners then developed other questions, such as follow-up questions or other sets of questions to ask; they also developed plans for making use of the information attained.

Demonstration of Mastery

Mastery of the skill set (asking worthwhile questions, seeking answers, and verifying them) was demonstrated as answers were obtained and used to solve workplace problems.

Analysis of the Example

1. Was workplace performance actually improved through use of the skills taught in the course?

Several process improvements were made that demonstrably improved through-put or quality and reduced waste. The fact that the skills helped people obtain results sustained the motivation of the people in the course and of the managers who arranged for the course to be taught.

2. Was the question asking and utilization skill set the only one taught?

Asking questions and utilizing the answers was taught first (and described here) because it is a fundamental skill set that is quite valuable by itself and forms the foundation for many other Learning-to-Learn® skills. Work with question asking continued and was supported as other skills were learned.

3. What are the main skills in addition to question asking and utilization?

The major thinking skills (cognitive skills) are asking questions, generating answers, and checking answers. They occur as a three-part process: *question, answer, check.* Learning the skills involves becoming fluent in asking good questions, in generating plausible answers, and in checking to be sure the answers are "good" answers. A question fluency exercise would be, for example, asking as many questions as possible about a common object (a pencil, a chair, a telephone, a loaf of bread) in one minute. Another exercise would be asking as many questions as possible about one of the objects but from several different perspectives (a consumer, a producer, a chemist, an economist, a business person). A practical question fluency exercise might be asking five good questions about a technical article in thirty seconds or less. An answer fluency exercise might be generating three plausible answers to a question (e.g., "What are three strategies political party X might use to win the next election?" "What are three possible causes of low production on line Y?" "How might we improve the quality of vegetables grown in hothouses?") in one minute or less. An answer checking fluency exercise might be, given an article that discusses political strategy, determine which of the three strategies the author is recommending and state why it is recommended within three minutes. Another fluency exercise that uses all three skills would be to generate three questions that, answered, would summarize a twenty-page technical article, answer the three questions correctly, and generate three more detailed questions in X amount of time.

> • *Self-Assessment Question*: What are one or two important workplace problems that would be easier to solve if people were to become fluent in asking, answering, and checking?

4. Can the Learning-to-Learn® skills be applied to acquiring complex cognitive skills?

As an example, the skill set involved in writing a paragraph, when combined with the skill set involved in identifying the questions readers would have about an issue and the skill of asking organized sequences of questions enables people to write well-constructed memos. Learning-to-Learn® skills are combined in various ways to generate a variety of complex cognitive skills. Each skill set is mastered separately and then combined to generate more complex skills sets. Mastery of each skill set is demonstrated each time it is combined with another skill set.

An example of using one skill set to generate a more complex skill set would be using the questioning skills to generate a set of questions applicable to several subjects, for example five different businesses within an industry. Using the subjects as column headings and the questions as the rows yields a matrix which, when filled in, provides well-organized information. For example, the data for a term paper in a business course might be generated by identifying six key questions to ask to determine the potential of a business enterprise and then applying the questions to the five businesses. The matrix guides data collection; after the student has gathered the data to answer all the questions and fill in the thirty cells of the matrix, the student has the information needed to write an excellent paper. Each skill involved can be mastered readily, but the set of skills involved in gathering such data sets, breaking complex questions into question sequences, constructing paragraphs that answer question sequences, etc., enables a learner to write an analytical paper on a complex topic.

5. Why should designers of performance-based training be interested in Learning-to-Learn®?

Most jobs are continuously changing; many, perhaps most, are increasing in complexity. By teaching people how to learn, we are providing them with skills that will enable them to keep up with the changes and, incidentally, saving organizations enormous amounts of money that would otherwise have to be spent on retraining.

> • *Self-Assessment Question*: What are one or two significant problems in public education that would become easier to solve if educators could and would actually help students learn-to-learn?

How PBI and Learning-to-Learn® Work Together

Specific Learning-to-Learn® skills can be taught through performance-based training (PBI) exercises; the Learning-to-Learn® skills, in turn, make the training more efficient and effective.

Guided Observation

Learning-to-Learn® skills, especially question-asking skills, are quite useful in guiding observation and in guiding analytic thinking. That is why scientific research focuses on specific research questions; why philosophical and humanistic inquiry focus on and revolve around questions; why determining training needs revolves around questions; why evaluation, troubleshooting, and problem solving revolve around questions.

Guided Practice

Questions can be used to guide practice, for example: "As you read the manual, find clear answers to these questions: . . ." "Use these questions to guide your problem-solving practice: . . ."

Demonstration of Mastery

In academic learning, mastery is typically demonstrated by answering questions, e.g., by taking tests, answering questions in discussions, or by writing papers that address good questions. Performance also can be evaluated for mastery by use of a checklist of questions: "Did the salesperson greet the customer within three minutes?" "Ask leading questions about the merchandise the customer was looking at?" Mastery of attitudes can also be evaluated through checklists of questions: "Did the person approach the problem constructively?" "Offer balanced criticism?" "Match deeds to words?" "Display emotions that were consistent with the attitude?" Knowing the types of questions (about content, skill criteria, or attitude) can guide learners, not only in learning but also in displaying what they have learned.

> • *Self-Assessment Questions*: In what situations have people misjudged your attitude? What did they see that lead them to their opinions? What did you see that led you to make a different judgment? How could you have displayed your thoughts, feelings, and actions differently so that people would have been more likely to judge your attitude accurately? On reflection, is it surprising that managers or trainers, seeing imperfect displays of thoughts, feelings, or actions often misread attitudes?

How Learning-to-Learn® Works in Three Domains of Learning

Educational psychologists have identified three domains of learning: *cognitive, affective,* and *psychomotor.* The cognitive domain can be seen as *knowledge,* the psychomotor as *skills,* and the affective as *attitudes, feelings, or emotions.* The domains work together, as when we feel good when we think we do something well, but they have different dynamics and different neural and chemical bases. The cognitive domain (knowing) deals with material that is, primarily, mediated by the quick-acting central nervous system. The psychomotor domain (doing) deals with material that is, primarily, mediated by the slower-acting striated muscles. The affective domain (feelings) deals with material that is, primarily, mediated by the even-slower-acting smooth muscles and glands.

Cognitive-domain procedures for learning emphasize the question/answer/check process:

- *Guided Observation*: asking questions to identify key concepts, principles, or variables present
- *Guided Practice*: generating answers to questions about concepts, principles, or variables and organizing the answers
- *Demonstration of Mastery:* checking adequacy of answers against other knowledge and against specific intellectual criteria or standards

Psychomotor-domain procedures involve action learning:

- *Guided Observation*: asking questions such as "Where are we going?" "How shall we get there?" and "How will we know we've arrived?" or "Why is this important?" "What's it all about?" and "How do we do it?"
- *Guided Practice*: practice with feedback
- *Demonstration of Mastery*: mastering specific skills for specific criterion levels and then combining them with other skills in a skill set

Affective-domain procedures involve emotional or attitudinal learning:

- *Guided Observation*: identifying situations in which an emotion or attitude occurs, interpreting the emotional significance of the situations, and identifying appropriate and inappropriate interpretations and actions
- *Guided Practice*: practice in using new interpretations and acting in accord with them
- *Demonstration of Mastery*: continuing the practice until feeling natural, confident, and successful

---

- *Self-Assessment Questions*: Thinking, feeling, and doing are intertwined in adult learners. How is a learner likely to feel after successfully going through a question/answer/check sequence to learn something new and valuable? after generating an answer but being unsure of its accuracy and having no way to check it? after learning something new but feeling that it is worthless?

> - How can asking questions (a cognitive-domain activity) guide observation and practice in skill learning? (The "psych" in psychomotor refers to cognition; technically, the term means "cognitively guided motor learning.")
> - How can asking questions guide observation in the affective domain?

Guided Observation

Notice that the phases of performance-based instruction (observation, practice, mastery) apply to all three domains. Imagine that learners, early in performance-based instruction, go on a tour of the workplace. The guidance before the tour can emphasize one or more of the three domains:

- *Cognitive/knowledge domain*: Ask them questions about how they know what to do!
- *Affective/attitude domain*: Ask them questions about why what they do is important and how they feel about their work!
- *Psychomotor/skill domain*: Observe how people do their jobs. Ask them about the procedures!

Similar questions can be asked in discussions during or after the tour, e.g., "What are some of the principles or guidelines you saw in operation?" "What did you see people do?" "What did they seem to like about their work?" "What could they tell you about why their work is important?" The questions can be used to guide attention to one or all three domains.

Guided Practice

Questions used to guide practice can probe one or more of the three domains:

- *Cognitive/knowledge domain*: "As you read the manual, try to find clear answers to these questions:. . . ." "What questions are you using to guide your trouble shooting?"
- *Affective/attitude domain*: "How do you feel about your progress?" "Do you feel that you have done enough for now?" "You seem to be gaining confidence. Is this true?" "You seem frustrated. Is that right?"
- *Psychomotor/skill domain*: "Are you still having to think about what you are doing or is it becoming more automatic?" "Are you close to the performance standards you've set for this practice session?"

Demonstration of Mastery

Mastery, if the truth were told, must involve all three domains. Learners must know what they are doing and why they are doing it, they must be able to do it quickly and well, and they must be confident in and feel good about what they are doing. But mastery of all three domains tends to be assessed differently:

- In academic/cognitive learning, mastery is typically demonstrated by how many answers one can give to a series of questions
- In skill learning, mastery is typically demonstrated one isolated skill at a time
- In affective learning, mastery is typically not measured at all, although people attempt to measure it by cognitive methods such as ratings or anonymous questionnaires

That might be one of the reasons mastery is experienced as infrequently as it is. We simply do not test for it and, thereby, fail to know when it occurs.

One reason people do not successfully assess mastery in all three domains is that the domains have different time dimensions. It is much easier to learn, cognitively, how to interpret a control chart than it is to become skillful at identifying patterns; it is much easier to describe the standards for high quality performance than it is to acquire the skills necessary to perform to those standards; and it takes longer still to feel comfortable or confident while performing to standards.

Tips and Caveats

1. Using questions to guide learning and mastery demonstrations can be effective, but it must be done wisely. If we guide learning of content with narrow or shallow questions, we lead learners toward a narrow or shallow understanding or toward displaying useless skills or phony attitudes. It is important for both learners and instructors to learn how to ask good questions.

2. The major breakthrough of recent research in the cognitive sciences, from the perspective of education, training, and HRD, is that cognitive skills are skills. They can be studied, analyzed, and developed in the same way as other skills. Older approaches that had tried to strengthen cognitive skills simply by exercising them did not work. Exercise does not work, but guided practice does: Specific performance goals, planned variations, and feedback are the keys.

3. Cognitive skills, as defined by leading cognitive scientists, are quite specific, indeed they can often be made extremely specific and simulated by computer programs (Simon, 1988). The point is that learning to learn is effective only when there is guided practice of specific skills that result in specific products,

e.g., problem definitions, solution alternatives, informative memos, and analytic papers.

4. One limitation of transfer of training is that too many training programs put in too much cognitive material, leaving time for too little skill practice and sending people out with too little skill to use on the job. "Knowing about" is faster than skill in performing, and confidence can come later. Skill lags behind cognition and affect lags behind skill.

5. People are concerned about measuring attitudes verbally for fear that people might lie to look good or manipulate a performance rating. The concern is justified, but we can still measure attitudes by observation: Actions truly speak louder than words. If people frequently choose to do something in their free time, they probably like doing it. If people act motivated for a long period of time, they probably are. If people act as though they like the job or respect minority people or divergent viewpoints, and do so for long periods of time, they probably do. To be sure, attitudes and emotions can be faked, but it is not easy.

6. A genuine dilemma must be overcome by HRD people who want to help people learn to learn. One horn of the dilemma is that acquiring proficiency in skills requires much guided practice; it does not happen overnight. The other horn of the dilemma is that few people will practice for long if they are not attaining specific results. One must assure that the guided practice is directed toward accomplishing something of immediate value to the learner. Skill sets that produce immediate results will be learned and used; skill sets that do not produce immediate results will not be used. If they require extensive practice to learn, they will be learned by very few people.

7. The practice exercises below provide several examples of how to immediately apply skill sets. Many more examples are included in Heiman & Slomianko (1993; 1994).

Practice Exercises

Guided Observation Exercise One

1. Think about people you work with who have reputations for being "intelligent" or "analytical" or "good problem solvers." Listen to the questions these people ask. Write down questions until you have a list of twenty or so. Also write down some of the questions other people ask, emphasizing questions that seem "different" or "off target."

2. Review the questions: Would you say that the people you selected typically ask more or better questions than other people? Organize their good questions into three to five categories, if possible.

3. Decide whether asking such questions would help a person to become well informed, to find the facts, to learn about problems and issues.

Guided Observation Exercise Two

1. Find opportunities to observe a group engaged in problem solving. If possible, select a group that uses a trained facilitator or has a skillful leader.
2. Observe the group. Listen to the questions people ask, especially when the group seems to be having good and constructive interchanges. Write some of the questions down. Listen carefully at times when the group seems to be stuck. Identify questions that keep them stuck. Identify questions people ask that help the group start moving again.
3. Review the questions that seem to facilitate the process when things are going well; review the questions that help a group become stuck or unstuck. What can you conclude about the importance of questions in leading or facilitating groups?

Guided Practice Exercise One

1. Identify a recurring problem or discomfort you face at work.
   - Generate a few questions about the problem or reasons why it should be solved.
   - Identify one or more persons who would be good sources of answers and ask them the questions.
   - Write a statement describing the problem and state reasons why it should be solved. Check with the person(s) interviewed, asking "Does this seem right to you?"
2. After the purpose of the effort is clarified, generate a list of questions that, if answered, would help you complete the assignment or project.
3. Seek answers. Act on them, generating and having other questions answered as necessary. Document the process by keeping a record of the questions asked and answered.
4. Reflect on how using the questions enabled you to focus your attention and obtain information. Which questions were most useful? least useful? What were you most comfortable with about the process? least comfortable?
5. Make some notes about how you could do another project more efficiently or effectively.
6. Make notes about how you could help specific people to learn skills involving asking, answering, checking, verifying, or using answers.
7. Plan a second project in which you improve your use of learning skills while helping others to improve their learning skills.

Guided Practice Exercise Two

1. Identify a new assignment, new challenge, or project at work.
   - Generate one to three questions about the purpose of the new assignment.
   - Identify one or more persons who would be good sources of answers and ask the questions.
   - Write a statement describing the purpose of the assignment or project. Get back to the person(s) interviewed asking, "Does this seem right to you?"
2. Once the purpose of the effort has been clarified, generate a list of questions that, if answered, would help you complete the assignment or project.
3. Seek answers. Act on them, generating and having other questions answered as necessary. Document the process by keeping a record of the questions asked and answered.
4. Continue the process of asking and clarifying and answering and acting and reflecting, etc., until you have completed the assignment.

Guided Practice Exercise Three

1. Review Chapter Ten on needs assessment. Identify the major questions to be asked during a needs assessment.
2. Practice using the questions during the next needs assessment you do *or* modify the questions so that they would work for a problem-solving activity you do.

Guided Practice Exercise Four

1. Review Chapter Eleven on the structured-design process. Identify the major questions being asked during the process.
2. Practice using some of the questions during any instructional-design work you do *or* modify the questions so that they would work for a problem-solving activity you do.
3. Do the same for Chapter Twelve on integrating evaluation. Because there are so many questions in Chapter Twelve, select only a few at a time to work with.

Guided Practice Exercise Five

1. Obtain a copy of *Smart Questions: A New Strategy for Successful Managers* (Leeds, 1987) or a similar book.

2. Select some of the questions sets in it.
3. Practice using them.
4. After each practice session, ask yourself these questions (and act on the answers):
   - What worked well?
   - What did not?
   - On the whole, did I obtain the information I wanted?
   - What should I do now, based on the information?
   - How can I do better next time?

Guided Practice Exercise Six

1. Obtain a copy of one or both of these books: *Success in College and Beyond* (Heiman & Slomianko, 1993) or *Learning-to-Learn®: Critical Thinking Skills for the Quality Workforce* (Heiman & Slomianko, 1994).
2. Select at least one exercise from one of the books and do it.
3. Do additional exercises, selecting those that have specific and immediate application in your personal or professional life.

Guided Practice Exercise Seven

1. Identify a group of people or target population that would benefit from learning-to-learn.
2. Use one of the books above as the basis for a course.
3. Run the course and evaluate it.

Demonstrations of Mastery

Every few months, make a list of the seven most useful questions you know. Practice using them carefully and systematically and monitor the results. Notice how much the questions change from time to time and whether you begin asking very general questions that can be specifically tailored to a wide variety of situations. Such questions are powerful indeed, and a sure sign that you are learning to learn!

Mastery, of course, is obtained only with sufficient guided practice. Because practice in performance-based instruction is always guided toward achieving specific results, small successes can be demonstrated along the way. As you do the practice exercises and other projects, track your results, using Figure 13.1.

FIGURE 13.1. DEMONSTRATIONS OF MASTERY.

Project	Goal	Start	End	Results

APPENDIX

USER'S MANUAL FOR PERFORMANCE-BASED INSTRUCTION: LINKING TRAINING TO BUSINESS RESULTS

Dale Brethower & Karolyn Smalley

Introduction

Training is unavoidable, costly, and sometimes extremely valuable:

- Unavoidable because people learn, for better or worse, as they work
- Costly because time spent learning is taken away from time doing work
- Valuable because it sometimes improves performance and avoids mistakes, delays, and lost opportunities due to lack of knowledge or skill

The performance-based instruction techniques described in this book assure that training and other HRD projects will be more valuable than costly.

Structure of the Book

The book is written to be used by practicing HRD professionals and by people who are learning about human resource development in an academic setting.

Each chapter is focused on specific techniques that can be applied immediately in the workplace, providing practice exercises for HRD professionals and professionals-in-training. The practice exercises are difficult for full-time students who are not in a setting in which they are involved in ongoing training programs. They are also difficult for HRD professionals because their plates are typically full already; they do not have much time or many opportunities to try something new. However, finding time to do the practice exercises is extremely important, as it takes significant amounts of guided practice to attain expertise with complex skills (as any accomplished musician, athlete, attorney, physician, or HRD professional knows). This short User's Manual is meant to share experiences and ideas about not only how to learn about performance-based instruction by reading the book but also how to become proficient through guided practice.

The Structure of the User's Manual

Every reader of the book is unique in terms of prior knowledge, skills, and attitudes, in terms of current circumstances, and in terms of future goals and aspirations. However, we have provided only three sets of suggestions for use, as though there are only three categories of users: HRD managers and their staffs, instructors and students in academic institutions, and rugged individualists.

HRD Managers and Staff

Suggestions in the abstract miss the mark so we have constructed a specific scenario.

Scenario: The HRD manager is employed within a large organization. Some people in the organization understand HRD well and have been good partners in HRD projects over the years. Others have depressingly high expectations of HRD, expecting that it can, almost overnight, prepare a training event that is a marvel of effectiveness and joy. Others have depressingly low expectations of HRD, believing that it exemplifies HR's ability to make the simple complex and the needed unattainable.

Eight HRD specialists make up the staff. Five were there when the HRD manager arrived and mildly resent anything innovative the HRD manager suggests. Three were recruited by the HRD manager and have good potential but little HRD experience. Three of the eight, including one of the three new staff members (recruited from within the organization), understand organizational politics reasonably well. Most of the staff members say the words "organizational politics" as if they were sucking on a lemon, not realizing that organizations have to have informal organizational structures to balance out and compensate for deficiencies in the formal structures.

The HRD manager is interested in the performance-improvement emphasis espoused by many in the field, including influential members of the American Society for Training and Development (ASTD) and International Society for Performance Improvement (ISPI).

The HRD manager first looked at the Table of Contents and looked through the book, seeking to determine just what practical techniques are in each chapter. Figure UM.1 shows what she discovered. Intrigued but cautious, she sketched out a plan.

1. Use some of the ideas in Chapter Eight to "continuously improve" the coaching course. Because I still teach it some of the time, so that won't make waves. Might try the same thing with the conflict-management course, either instead of or in addition to coaching.

2. Talk to Sally [one of the new staffers] to see if she would be interested in using the techniques in Chapter Two to set up some on-the-job training. It would help her gain some exposure to line operations and make some inroads out in Sanderson's area, where there are a lot of new hires, partly because turnover is too high. Might get Sanderson off my back about the "morale-building" program he thinks he needs. I'll have Sally do some needs-assessment stuff from Chapter Ten; maybe I should start with that. Better talk to Sanderson before I talk to Sally.

3. If things work out OK with Sally, I'll begin talking to the other new people about developmental plans like those in Chapter Four. Their developmental plans will include doing some of the other chapters, so they'll be doing more and more performance-based instruction.

4. After I've worked the bugs out of the Chapter Four stuff, figuring out how to make it work here with the new people, I'll approach Stan. He's the most progressive of the old-timers—in fact, there is a quite a bit of performance-based stuff in some of the programs he likes the most; he likes action-training projects and probably would do more of that if he had the green light. Stan would probably like Chapter Eight if I could figure out how to position it with him so he doesn't think I'm attacking all the work he's done in the past.

The HRD manager, wisely, thought about the capabilities and interests of staff, the needs and wants and potential for acceptance by customers, and how to do things one step at a time.

FIGURE UM.1. OUTLINE OF USAGE IDEAS.

	Chapter	Contains Techniques for
	Part One: Performance-Based Instruction: A Practical Approach to Training Issues	
1	Performance-Based Instruction: Application to Customer Service	Enabling new, seasonally hired people to move up to speed quickly, performing accurately and responsively
2	Performance-Based Instruction On the Job	Designing, implementing, and managing OJT that brings people up to speed quickly and yields documentation of the job learned
3	Performance-Based Teamwork Training	Establishing problem-solving teams and using the solving of real problems as a vehicle for teamwork training
4	Performance-Based Development	Using individual development projects to achieve current goals and develop people for the future
5	Performance-Based Instruction and the Hawthorne Effect	Establishing feedback plus on-the-job coaching and support as a training design and to assure transfer
6	Performance-Based Instruction and Job Aids	Using job aids as a training tool and as performance support for any training
	Part Two: Performance-Based Instruction: A Paradigm for the Twenty-First Century	
7	Performance-Based Instruction: A Paradigm for Twenty-First-Century HRD	Describing the performance-based instruction paradigm, comparing it to familiar paradigms, the general education paradigm and the vocational education paradigm as well as "typical" training approaches
8	Converting to Performance-Based Instruction	Improving existing training programs by converting them, bit by bit, to performance-based instruction
9	Transfer of Training: Linking Training Events to What Happens Before and After	Making the linkages between prior knowledge, current learning, and workplace applications to support transfer of training
10	Needs Assessment and Performance-Based Instruction	Rapidly identifying performance gaps and causes thereof so that training will result in on-the-job performance improvements
11	A Structured-Design Approach for Performance-Based Instruction	Supporting the entire ADIE process with a set of worksheets usable by one person or a team, for small projects or large ones
12	Integrating Evaluation into Performance-Based Instruction	Using specific evaluation questions to assure that each part of the ADIE process is conducted in ways that reduce design time and increase impact
13	Performance-Based Instruction and Learning-to-Learn®	Supporting rapid learning of specific content and enhancing learning skills to assure continuing learning on the job and in future training or education

There are many other creative ways to use the techniques and practice exercises in the book. All it takes is good judgment about where to start, with whom, and how rapidly to move ahead:

- The HRD manager might have decided to use the structured-design approach from Chapter Eleven with one of the staffers. The chapter provides an efficient hands-on way to work with someone to coach him or her through a project. It would work best with someone who likes to work in a very orderly way or who does not really know how to do a training project from start to finish.
- Or the training manager might have worked with one of the "old" staff to use material from Chapter Twelve to evaluate some of the programs run by vendors or designed in-house far enough in the past so that it would make sense to reevaluate and redesign the programs.
- Another HRD manager might decide that the performance-based instruction approach is enough of a departure from what his clientele expects of training so that he should devise a plan for selling the approach to key decision makers in the organization. (Notice that the HRD manager above used that tactic to sell the approach to them.) One way to do that would be to devote some staff meetings to these questions:
  —Are we delivering the products and services we believe are best for the company?
  —What are our best and worst products or services?
  —What should we do more of and less of?

A group problem-solving process similar to that shown in Chapter Three could be used to assure that the staff meetings were productive. Once the HRD staff, whatever size, is clear about answers to those questions, other questions would emerge quite naturally:

- How can we "sell" the products or services we believe are the most beneficial to people and to the company?
- Who are our best prospects for "buying" the best we have to offer?
- How can we approach each prospect?
- How would the product/service benefit the prospect?
- How can we approach each prospect?

The process of developing performance-based instruction begins with the identification of a performance-improvement opportunity, i.e., with a search for benefits to the organization. The process illustrated in several of the chapters and shown in full in Chapter Eleven is, with a little tweaking, a sales process.

Part of the tweaking is to establish, beforehand, which projects should be given priority, e.g., projects focused on the revenue side of the business or projects for a specific prospective champion. Additional tweaking might be required to assure that the analyst always keeps the clients' interest in focus. A client might perceive a real need for three hours of training, delivered very quickly, on a specific topic. The HRD manager might "close the sale" by agreeing to deliver that amount on that topic at an early date. A question such as "In addition, what results would you like to see from the training?" will determine whether or not there is an opportunity to make the training event more performance-based.

Many sales processes, ranging from selling cars to selling clothes, begin by closing the sale of a basic product or service, then selling accessories; structuring their product or service line to assure that there is money to be made in accessories. Selling people what they want to buy, then adding on what you want to sell or believe they really need is quite appropriate. Good salespeople know that some customers want to buy a basic item and be done with it, whereas others want to be educated about options and given an opportunity to buy something that will serve them better. That is true whether the customer is in a duty-free zone with an airplane to catch in ten minutes or whether the customer is looking for a new house or seeking performance improvement through training.

- Another HRD manager could use the text to help deal with everyday challenges, such as the ones shown in the job aid in Figure UM.2.

Instructors and Students in Academic Settings

Again, we have constructed a specific scenario.

Scenario: This scenario is patterned after the use of the book by one of the authors in a graduate-level course. The course serves approximately twenty-five graduate students per class, drawn from several different graduate programs. It typically meets for three hours once per week for fifteen weeks. The book is the main text, supplemented by lectures describing the state-of-the-art in HRD. Typically, chapters are assigned in sequence. Chapter One is intended as a starting point, but the other chapters could be assigned in other sequences to match student needs, to match a text, or to suit an instructor's preference.

In a typical class session:

1. Groups of four or five students discuss the material in one chapter. They have prepared by finding three items in the chapter that they like and two questions they have about the chapter—something they did not understand, disagree with, or believe would make a good examination question for the material.

During the first part of the discussion, each student lists the three items he or she liked and states why they were useful, enlightening, interesting, or whatever. Students then share their questions, clarifying the material if possible, and asking the instructor for input, if desired. Fifteen to twenty minutes are allotted for this discussion.

2. Students continue the discussion, emphasizing the self-assessment questions in the text. Another fifteen to twenty minutes are allotted.
3. Groups report on their discussions, bringing out meaningful points from the chapter, raising unresolved questions, sharing potential essay questions, and describing potential applications.
4. Reports and class discussion require another thirty minutes.
5. After a break there is a lecture, often (but not always) correlated with the material in the chapter and often (but not always) under thirty minutes in length.
6. The class ends with a work period in which task groups (of two or three people) plan their homework assignments—doing one or more of the practice exercises—and review their completed homework assignment from the previous chapter. Task groups and discussion groups have little overlap in membership. The former are set up so that people can communicate during the week. The distribution of labor, typically, is to discuss what the practice exercise will be, brainstorm and plan, and assign one group member to prepare the written document, in consultation with others as needed. One group member drafts an evaluation: "What's good about the work?" "How could it be improved?" The evaluation is turned in as part of the assignment.

In addition to the weekly homework assignments, each student is required to formulate a personal plan for professional development, based on the material in Chapter Four. For most of the students, the professional-development plan deals with HRD and gaining more proficiency in the topics covered by each chapter. Students on other career paths develop plans appropriate to their professional goals.

Facilitation of in-class discussions follows a pattern that is intended to support critical thinking and open communication, so the instructor:

1. Leads the applause after student presentations to acknowledge their work.
2. Supports the reports of key points and of obstacles by providing additional examples to illustrate the students' points or show support through directed questions.
3. Asks questions, e.g., "Why is that point important?" "What do you see as (other) obstacles to using these techniques?" "What suggestions do you have for overcoming the obstacles?"

FIGURE UM.2. JOB AID FOR DEALING WITH DAILY CHALLENGES.

Situation	Analysis	Action
Your organization has spent a lot of money on team training; there are rumblings and grumblings that it hasn't helped much.	You know of two areas in which it has helped improve performance and several areas in which there has been no management effort to support teamwork.	Use the material in Chapters Three and Eight to help redesign some of the teamwork training; use the material in Chapter Nine to help establish linkages that will support transfer of training.
People say you should do some team training; everyone else is doing it.	You believe there are a few areas of the company in which team training would help and several in which it wouldn't work. There's strong pressure from a senior vice president to get something going.	1. Arrange for a vendor to bring in a canned course, paying for it with chargebacks. 2. Send out a brochure on external team training opportunities. 3. Advertise a team work training program that you will make available to any department that wants to train the whole department. Use the material in Chapter Three to design the training. Use the material in Chapter Ten to help interested managers focus on what they want to accomplish if they send their whole department.
Several vendors have offered to do team training for you; you wonder whether you could do it better in house and wonder how you could get the most mileage out of it if you hire a vendor.	A cost comparison shows significant variations among vendors. Telephone interviews show a significant variation in willingness to tailor the training to your company.	Use a set of evaluation questions taken from the material in Chapter Twelve to help you select a vendor who is open to evaluation and to tailoring the course to achieve specific performance improvement goals.
There's a lot of talk in your organization about "learning organizations" and people seem to think you should be doing something.	You believe most of it is just talk, but there's an opportunity to do something with one or two key managers.	Use the material in Chapter Three as an example of how small task forces could be "learning organizations," and material in Chapter Thirteen to support "personal mastery." Discuss a problem-solving project as a way to start with one or both of the managers.
There are problems in the workplace that some believe are due to weaknesses in basic reading and arithmetic skills.	You believe that there are definite weaknesses in basic skills but that much of the difficulty can be traced to lack of clear guidance.	1. Use the material in Chapter Ten to analyze the situation further. 2. Use material in Chapter Five to establish better guidance. 3. Use material in Chapter Thirteen to train the people weak in basic skills in how to ask questions and find the on-the-job help they need. 4. Seek

FIGURE UM.2. CONTINUED

Situation	Analysis	Action
		a vendor who uses performance-based literacy and numeracy instruction and/or offers validation data.
You are in charge of a training operation that is evaluated on usage: how many people spend how many hours in training courses.	You believe that if you switched abruptly to performance-based instruction, you'd soon look worse on those measures. You also believe that if you continue to be evaluated on how much you spend rather than how much you contribute, you'll be vulnerable to budget cuts.	1. Use material in Chapter Eight to move some of your popular courses closer to performance-based instruction while maintaining enrollments in those courses. 2. Design new courses as performance-based instruction whenever you can. 3. Use material in Chapter Two to increase the amount of OJT you do, increasing your numbers that way.
You want to reposition your HRD function from a training emphasis to a performance-improvement emphasis.	You believe you should build significant support from customers as a first step.	1. Visit key managers and offer to do more OJT for their new people. 2. Use material in Chapter Twelve to help you document the effectiveness of the OJT in terms of bringing people up to speed quickly. 3. Visit key managers and encourage them to talk about the challenges they are currently facing. Offer to help, using material from whichever chapter seems most appropriate.
One of your stand-up trainers is interested in what happens to people after training.	You see this as an opportunity to develop the person and to begin doing more follow-up support for your courses.	Use the material in Chapter Nine to discover what to look for and material in Chapter Twelve to help the person do follow-up evaluation.
One of your stand-up trainers keeps "redesigning" the courses as she presents them.	Some of the redesigns are improvements, and you see this as an opportunity to develop the person and to build more elements of performance-based instruction into course offerings.	Use the material in Chapter Eight to guide redesign of a couple of courses. If the person continues to be interested in design, have the person do a project using the material in Chapter Eleven.
One of your designers keeps complaining about inability to gain access to subject-matter experts.	You see this as an opportunity to develop the person and move from content-driven to performance-based instruction.	1. Have the person make job aids based on what some of the best performing people are doing, and then interview subject-matter experts to evaluate the job aids. 2. Have the person *not* ask what content is needed but rather ask the experts to evaluate the guided practice and demonstration of mastery exercise drafts.

4. Comments on the quality of the obstacles, e.g., "I'm delighted that you see the obstacles so clearly; if not, you could be blind-sided." "Would that obstacle be important for other approaches to HRD?" and of the key points, e.g., "I'm delighted that you see that point so clearly; if you did not, it would not be performance-based instruction." "Do other approaches to HRD have that same feature?"
5. Summarizes the key points the students have made or asks one of them to summarize.

Problems

Many students have been trained by instructors to be obsequious and by peers not to show enthusiasm. The facilitation style is an attempt to create an open atmosphere, which is easier to do in small seminars than with a class of twenty to thirty students, but it is worth doing. Perhaps I overdo it; students are astounded near the end of the course when I occasionally answer a question directly rather than reflecting it back to the class or giving alternatives. (I offer to give my opinion on issues if they want it—but they do not ask very often.)

There are two problems specific to using the book in an academic course. The first stems from the practical nature of the material: it does not emphasize theory and research findings and does not attempt to present a balanced view of the HRD field. Instead, it focuses on HRD that has, as its purpose, improvement of performance related to current or strategic organizational performance goals.

This problem can be dealt with by using a companion text, using this book as a set of application cases and exercises. It takes about an hour a week for a typical student to read a chapter, perhaps another hour to think about it, and only a bit more to draft a homework exercise for a task group. It would be possible to assign additional reading, either from a companion text or from a collection of current articles. The problem can also be dealt with through supplementary lectures.

The second problem is more difficult: the book is itself performance-based instruction, which is a drawback in a traditional academic environment in which most students are not currently working to implement training projects. The book works well as performance-based instruction for working students but not for full-time students.

Here are two good ways to deal with the mismatch between the academic world and the world of work:

1. Sometimes at least one student in the group is working and can obtain permission to do a small project at work. That student serves as the "client" for

the week, another student acts as the HRD specialist and prepares material for a practice exercise, and the other acts as evaluator.

2. More often, none of the students is in a position to serve as "client" for the topic at hand. In that case, I simply ask the students to create a fictitious scenario and do a simulated project. Students can create a very rich scenario and have fun doing it. The work they produce provides a model for guidance and inspiration when they have an opportunity to do a real project.

The students tend to use the same setting from week to week for their fictitious scenarios, which I encourage. They use a small business of a type with which they are all familiar, e.g., a neighborhood convenience store, a retail store in a mall, a restaurant, or a medical clinic. They build an increasingly rich scenario during the term. Some do informational interviews in real organizations to obtain realistic details for their scenarios.[1]

I also guide concept-fluency and question-fluency exercises about once per week in the second half of the term. Groups of five students (the discussion groups) are asked to write down as many concepts, ideas, principles, or key items as they can in three minutes. They report the total number of concepts generated by the group as well as the raw totals. The groups generate more and more concepts from week to week and begin noticing that concepts "flow" in clusters. A variant of the exercise is to begin with a specific topic, e.g., "List all the concepts you can think of relevant to finding business issues or performance gaps," "List all the concepts you can think of or relate to obstacles to performance-based instruction," or "List all the concepts you would have to use to give a good answer to this question: What are the most likely causes of *important* performance deficiencies in an organization?" (I change the question with each round of the exercise.)

The concept-fluency exercises enable students to notice that they are learning a lot and to organize their knowledge into useful clusters. I learned the technique from Dr. Ogden Lindsley. According to him, concept lists in response to questions correlate about 0.80 with essay answers written to the same questions.

Question-fluency exercises are similar to the concept-fluency exercises except that I ask groups to "shout out" the questions (within their groups) to minimize writing time. I use question fluency in part because good HRD professionals must fluently ask a great many questions and in part because I want students to do well on the written final exam, which is constructed from questions I collect from the question-fluency exercises. Students report the number of different questions their groups generated, along with the "most interesting" question they generated. Over time, more "interesting" questions are generated, as students notice that interesting questions tend to be ones that have several smaller questions embedded in them and that the questions enable them to integrate the material in meaningful ways.

The concept-fluency and question-fluency exercises serve an important instructional purpose and can be fun to do as students devise tactics for generating more, engage in competitions with other groups or their own group's previous best, applaud one another's work, and try stretching the limits of relevance of the concepts they list. Facilitation is directed at improving fluency and having fun.

The next time I teach the course I might require task groups to do Guided Observation Exercises, requiring them to do some minimum number during the term, because students who elect to do them report that they enjoy and learn from them. The requirement might be a burden in a course that requires a substantial amount of reading from a standard text or supplementary materials.

Many, probably most students at Western Michigan University have liked the practical nature of the material, but find it frustrating that they are unable to practice enough to really master the techniques. We deal with that difficulty openly; they are perfectly aware that other approaches have other drawbacks and some find this drawback a refreshing change of pace.

Other Approaches

The detailed scenario above is not intended to suggest that this is the only way to use the text in a course. The intention is to give enough details to show one way to use it and spark creative variations. For example, one way to use the book would be as a supplement in which students are asked to read, let us say, the first chapters in Parts One and Two, then browse through the others to find an application that they want to develop. They would do a project worth 20 percent of the total grade, with another 10 percent allocated to an evaluation paper they would write, evaluating the project in terms of the other material they learned in the course.

Rugged Individualists

Rugged individualists can just dive in and use the book as seems best. Slightly less rugged individualists can scan the book to find the chapter most closely related to their current work responsibilities and begin there. Here are some possibilities:

1. Recruit a mentor and begin with Chapter Four, consulting with the mentor for ideas and support.
2. Use an existing course that is working well as the vehicle. Apply the techniques in Chapter Eight to continuously improving it.

3. Use an existing course that is a problem. Apply the techniques in Chapter Eleven to rethink the course and redesign it.
4. Play with the checklists in Chapter Ten, either using them to critique training activities or to design evaluation of a current project.
5. Read Chapter Seven and engage people in philosophical discussions about the content, using suggestions in the practice exercises.
6. Use material in Chapter Two to train yourself in how to do something.
7. Browse through the book, picking out Guided Observation Exercises that would be fun to do and do them.

If you decide not to recruit a mentor, perhaps the person you report to or someone else you respect, consider tracking your own performance carefully. Devise a project tracking form such as the one in Figure UM.3 or use some other device to track your progress. Call each thing you do a project, specify at least two goals for it (What should the project accomplish? What will you learn from it), enter a start date and an end date, and make some notes about how it went. Play the mentor role yourself at least once per month, reviewing what you are attempting and what you are accomplishing.

A Last Word

People learn as they do their work, learning good and bad ways of doing things, good and bad habits, and good and bad attitudes. That is true of trainees, training managers, instructors, and rugged individualists alike. We hope that the practice exercises, worksheets, job aids, and information in the book facilitate learning good ways, good habits, and constructive attitudes. That hope is realistic given the experiences of people we know who have used the worksheets and job aids during the last couple of decades.

Note

1. Dr. Laura Methot originated the technique while she was taking the course. I borrowed the idea from her.

FIGURE UM.3. DEMONSTRATIONS OF MASTERY.

Project	Goal	Start	End	Comments/Results

BIBLIOGRAPHY AND REFERENCES

Berryman, S.E. (1993). Learning for the workplace. *Review of Educational Research, 19,* 343–401.

Brethower, D.M. (1963). Task analysis: The crux of programming. In *North Central Reading Association Yearbook,* Minneapolis: NCRA.

Brethower, D.M. (1982). Teaching students to be scholars. *Journal of Learning Skills, 2*(1), 3–10.

Brethower, D.M. (1982). The total performance system. In R.M. O'Brien, A.M. Dickinson, & M.P. Rosow (Eds.), *Industrial behavior modification: A management handbook.* New York: Pergamon Press.

Brethower, D.M. (1990). Instruction: Does it mean creating intelligence? *Journal of College and Adult Reading and Learning, 1,* 19–31.

Brethower, D.M. (1993a). Strategic improvement of workplace competence I: Breaking out of the incompetence trap. *Performance Improvement Quarterly, 5*(2), 17–28.

Brethower, D.M. (1993b). Strategic improvement of workplace competence II: The economics of competence. *Performance Improvement Quarterly, 5*(2), 29–42.

Brethower, D.M. (1994). Institutionalized failure: The high costs of ignoring basic principles of learning and instruction. In *Performance technology—1994: Selected proceedings of the 32nd NSPI Conference.* Bloomington, IN: NSPI Publications, 355–364.

Brethower, D.M. (1995). Specifying a human performance technology knowledge base. *Performance Improvement Quarterly, 8*(2), 17–39.

Brethower, D.M., & Rummler, G.A. (1966, Sept/Oct). For improved work performance: Accentuate the positive. *Personnel,* (43).

Brethower, D.M., & Smalley, K.A. (1992a). Converting to performance-based instruction. *Performance & Instruction, 31*(4), 27–32.

Brethower, D.M., & Smalley, K.A. (1992b). Evaluating performance-based instruction. *Performance & Instruction, 31*(7), 33–40.

Brethower, D.M., & Smalley, K.A. (1992c). Performance and instruction: Assuring that learning occurs and transfers to the job. *Performance & Instruction, 31*(6), 38–43.

Brethower, D.M., & Smalley, K.A. (1992d). Performance-based instruction: Definition and examples. *Performance & Instruction. 31*(3), 36–40.

Brethower, D.M., & Smalley, K.A. (1992e). Performance-based instruction: A training paradigm for the 21st century. *Performance & Instruction, 31*(5), 26–31.

Brethower, D.M., & Smalley, K.A. (1992f). Research based design evaluation criteria. *Performance technology—1992: Selected proceedings of the 30th NSPI Conference.* Bloomington, IN: NSPI Publications, 27–36.

Brethower, D.M., & Smalley, K.A. (1993). Good training and bad: How to get agreement on what "good training" means. *Performance Technology—1993: Selected proceedings of the 31st NSPI Conference.* Washington, DC: ISPI.

Brethower, D.M., & Wittkopp, C.J. (1987). Performance engineering: SPC and the total performance system. *Journal of Organizational Behavior Management, 9,* 83–93.

Brinkerhoff, R.O. (1988). *Achieving results from training: How to evaluate human resource development to strengthen programs and increase impact.* San Francisco: Jossey-Bass.

Brinkerhoff, R.O., Brethower, D.M., Hluchyj, T., & Nowakowski, J.R. (1983). *Program evaluation: A practitioner's guide for trainers and educators, Vol. 1: Design manual.* The Hague: Kluwer-Nijhoff.

Brinkerhoff, R.O., & Dressler, D. (1990). *Productivity measurement: A guide for managers and evaluators.* Newbury Park, CA: Sage Publications.

Brinkerhoff, R.O., Formella, L., & Smalley, K. (1994). Total quality management training for white-collar workers. In J.J. Phillips (Ed.), *In action: Measuring return on investment.* Alexandria, VA: ASTD.

Brinkerhoff, R.O., & Gill, S.J. (1994). *The learning alliance: Systems thinking in human resource development.* San Francisco: Jossey-Bass.

Broad, M., & Newstrom, J. (1992). *Transfer of training: Action-packed strategies to ensure high payoff from training investments.* Reading, MA: Addison-Wesley.

Broadwell, M.M. (1986). *The supervisor and on-the-job training.* (3rd ed.). Reading, MA: Addison-Wesley.

Brown, M.G. (1989). Extending performance technology: How to improve performance with better data. *Performance & Instruction, 28*(3), 1–6.

Brown, M.G. (1990). You get what you measure: Engineering a performance measurement system. *Performance & Instruction, 29*(5), 11–16.

Carnevale, A.P., Gainer, L.J., & Meltzer, A.S. (1990). *Workplace basics training manual.* San Francisco: Jossey-Bass.

Carnevale, A.P., Gainer, L.J., & Schulz, E. (1990). *Training the technical work force.* San Francisco: Jossey-Bass.

Carnevale, A.P., Gainer, L.J., & Villet, J. (1990). *Training in America: The organization and strategic role of training.* San Francisco: Jossey-Bass.

Cascio, W.F. (1982). *Costing human resources: The financial impact of behavior in organizations.* New York: Van Nostrand Reinhold.

Daniels, A.C. (1989). *Performance management: Improving quality productivity through positive reinforcement.* (3rd ed.). Tucker: GA: Performance Management.

Dean, P.J. (Ed.). (1994). *Performance engineering at work.* Batavia, IL: International Board of Standards for Training, Performance, & Instruction.

Derry, S.J., & Murphy, D.A. (1986). Designing systems that train learning ability: From theory to practice. *Review of Educational Research, 56,* 1–39.

Dick, W., & Carey, L. (1990). *The systematic design of instruction.* (3rd ed.) New York: Harper-Collins.

Eickhoff, S.M. (1991). *Organizational development through the implementation of strategic plans.* Unpublished doctoral dissertation, Western Michigan University, Kalamazoo.

Fournies, F.F. (1978). *Coaching for improved work performance.* New York: Van Nostrand Reinhold.

Fredericksen, L.W. (Ed.). (1982). *Handbook of organizational behavior management.* New York: Wiley.

Gery, G. (1991). *Electronic performance support systems: How and why to remake the workplace through the strategic application of technology.* Boston: Weingarten Press.

Gilbert, T. (1996). *Human competence: Engineering worthy performance.* Washington, DC: International Society for Performance Improvement/HRD Press.

Glaser, R., & Bassok, M. (1989). Learning theory and the study of instruction. *Annual Review of Psychology, 40,* 630–666.

Harless, J.H. (1978). *Job aid for selection and construction of job aids.* Newman, GA: Harless Performance Guild.

Heiman, M. (1987). Learning to learn: A behavioral approach to improving thinking. In Perkins et al. (Eds.), *Thinking.* Hillsdale, NJ: Erlbaum.

Heiman, M. (1991). Learning to learn. In A. Costa (Ed.), *Developing minds: A resource book on thinking skills.* Washington, DC: Association for Supervision and Curriculum Development.

Heiman, M., & Slomianko, J. (1993). *Success in college and beyond.* Allston, MA: Learning to Learn®.

Heiman, M., & Slomianko, J. (1994). *Learning to learn: Critical thinking skills for the quality workforce.* Allston, MA: Learning to Learn®.

Horn, R.E. (1976). *How to write information mapping.* Lexington, MA: Information Resources.

Horn, R.E. (1989). *Mapping hypertext.* Lexington, MA: Lexington Institute.

Hupp, T., Polak, C., & Westgaard, O. (1995). *Designing work groups, jobs, and work flow.* San Francisco: Jossey-Bass.

Johnson, K.R., & Layng, T.V.J. (1994). Morningside model of generative instruction. In R. Gardner III, D.M. Sainato, J.O. Cooper, T.E. Heron, W.L. Heward, J. Eshleman, & T.A. Grossi, *Behavior analysis in education: Focus on measurably superior instruction.* Pacific Grove, CA: Brooks/Cole.

Johnson, D.W., & Johnson, F.P. (1994). *Joining together: Group theory and group skills.* (5th ed.). Boston: Allyn and Bacon.

Joint Committee on Standards for Educational Evaluation. (1981). *Standards for evaluation of educational programs, projects, and materials.* New York: McGraw-Hill.

Kaufman, R. (1992). *Strategic planning plus: An organizational guide.* (Rev. ed.) Newbury Park, CA: Sage Publications.

Kirkpatrick, D.L. (1976). *Evaluating training programs.* New York: McGraw-Hill.

Knowles, M. (1984). *The adult learner: A neglected species.* (3rd ed.). Houston: Gulf Publishing.

Knowles, M. (1986). *Using learning contracts: Practical approaches to individualizing and structuring learning.* San Francisco: Jossey-Bass.

Komatsu, N.B. (1990). *Expert performance: Designing on-the-job-learning.* National Alliance of Business.

Kopelman, R.E. (1986). *Managing productivity in organizations: A practical, people oriented approach.* New York: McGraw-Hill.

Langdon, D. (1995). *The new language of work.* Amherst, MA: HRD Press.

Leeds, D. (1987). *Smart questions: A new strategy for successful managers.* New York: Berkley Books.

Lincoln, J.F. (1951). *Incentive management: A new approach to human relationships in industry and business.* Cleveland, OH: Lincoln Electric.

Lindberg, R.A., & Cohn, T. (1972). *Operations auditing.* New York: AMACOM.

Lineberry, C.S., & Bullock, D.H. (1980). *Job aids.* Englewood Cliffs, NJ: Educational Technology.

Mager, R.F. (1997). *How to turn learners on without turning them off.* (3rd ed.). Atlanta, GA: Center for Effective Performance.

Mager, R.F., & Pipe, P. (1984). *Analyzing performance problems.* (2nd ed.). Belmont, CA: Pitman Management and Training.

Markle, S.M. (1990). *Designs for instructional designers.* (3rd ed.). Champaign, IL: Stipes.

Means, B., Chelemer, C., & Knapp, M.S. (Eds.) (1991). *Teaching advanced skills to at-risk students.* San Francisco: Jossey-Bass.

Miller, G.A. (1956). The magical number seven plus or minus two: Some limits on our capacity for processing information. *Psychological Review, 63,* 81–97.

Mouton, J.S., & Blake, R.R. (1984). *Synergogy: A new strategy for education, training, and development.* San Francisco: Jossey-Bass.

Murray, M., & Owen, M.A. (1991). *Beyond the myths and magic of mentoring: How to facilitate an effective mentoring program.* San Francisco: Jossey-Bass.

Nadler, L., & Nadler, Z. (1989). *Developing human resources.* (3rd ed.). San Francisco: Jossey-Bass.

Nelson, J. (1992). Job aids. In R. Kaufman, S. Thiagarajan, & P. MacGillis, *The guidebook for performance improvement.* San Francisco: Pfeiffer.

O'Brien, R.M., Dickinson, A.M., & Rosow, M.P. (Eds.). (1982). *Industrial behavior modification: A management handbook.* New York: Pergamon Press.

Odiorne, G.S., & Rummler, G.A. (1988). *Training and development: A guide for professionals.* Chicago: Commerce Clearing House.

Parsons, H.M. (1974). What happened at Hawthorne? *Science, 183,* 922–932.

Phillips, J.J. (Ed.). (1994). *In action: Measuring return on investment.* Alexandria, VA: ASTD.

Proctor, R.W., & Dutta, A. (1995). *Skill acquisition and human performance.* Thousand Oaks, CA: Sage.

Roethlisberger, F.J., & Dickson, W.J. (1939). *Management and the worker.* Cambridge, MA: Harvard University Press.

Rosow, J.M., & Zager, R. (1988). *Training—The competitive edge: Introducing new technology in the workplace.* San Francisco: Jossey-Bass.

Rossett, A., & Gautier-Downes, J. (1992). *A handbook of job aids.* San Francisco: Jossey-Bass/Pfeiffer.

Rummler, G.A., & Brache, A.P. (1992). Transforming organizations through human performance technology. In H.D. Stolovitch & E.J. Keeps (Eds.), *Handbook of human performance technology: A comprehensive guide for analyzing and solving performance problems in organizations.* San Francisco: Jossey-Bass.

Rummler, G.A., & Brache, A.P. (1995). *Improving performance: How to manage the white space on the organization chart.* (2nd ed.). San Francisco: Jossey-Bass.

Schultz, T.W. (1978). *Economic analysis of investment in education.* Washington, DC: National Institute of Education.

Seels, B., & Glasgow, Z. (1990). *Exercises in instructional design.* Columbus, OH: Merrill.

Senge, P.M. (1990). *The fifth discipline: The art and practice of the learning organization.* New York: Doubleday/Currency.

Simon, H.A. (1981). *The sciences of the artificial.* (2nd ed.). Cambridge, MA: MIT Press.

Simon, H.A. (1990). Invariants of human behavior. *Annual Review of Psychology, 41,* 1–20.

Simpson, E.J. (1966). The classification of educational objectives, psychomotor domain. *Illinois Teacher of Home Economics, 10,* 110–144.

Smith, D.E.P. (Ed.). (1961). *Learning to learn.* New York: Harcourt, Brace, & World.

Snyder, G. (1992, Summer). Morningside academy: A learning guarantee. *Performance Management Magazine, 10,* 29–35.

Stolovitch, H.D., & Keeps, E.J. (Eds). (1992). *Handbook of human performance technology: A comprehensive guide for analyzing and solving performance problems in organizations.* San Francisco: Jossey-Bass.

Stufflebeam, D.L., Foley, W.J., Gephart, W.J., Guba, E.G., Hammond, R.L., Merriman, H.O., & Provus, M.M. (1971). *Educational evaluation & decision making.* Bloomington, IN: Phi Delta Kappa.

Svenson, R., & Rinderer, M.J. (1992). *The training and development strategic plan workbook.* Upper Saddle River, NJ: Prentice-Hall.

Svenson, R., & Wallace, K. (1989). Performance technology: A strategic management tool. *Performance & Instruction, 29*(8), 1–7.

Taylor, F.W. (1967). The principles of scientific management. New York: Norton. (Originally published 1911)

Tiemann, P.W., & Markle, S.M. (1990). *Analyzing instructional content: A guide to instruction and evaluation.* Champaign, IL: Stipes.

Tosti, D. (1991). The world's first job aid. *Performance & Instruction, 30*(7), 8–10.

Tosti, D., & Jackson, S.F. (1992). Influencing others to act. In H.D. Stolovitch & E.J. Keeps (Eds.), *Handbook of human performance technology: A comprehensive guide for analyzing and solving performance problems in organizations.* San Francisco: Jossey-Bass.

Wales, C.E., Nardi, A.H., & Stager, R.A. (1986). *Professional decision-making.* Morgantown, WV: Center for Guided Design.

Wales, C.E., & Stager, R.A. (1978). *The guided design approach.* Englewood Cliffs, NJ: Educational Technology.

Whimbey, A. (1975). *Intelligence can be taught.* New York: Dutton.

Wydra, F. (1980). *Learner controlled instruction.* Englewood Cliffs, NJ: Educational Technology.

LIST OF FIGURES ON DISKETTE

 These figures are available on the diskette enclosed at the back of the book. The figures are provided in two different formats, PDF and RTF. The PDF version allows you to print the figures *exactly* as they appear in the book. PDF files can be opened with Adobe® Acrobat® Reader available for free from the Adobe Systems Incorporated internet site www.adobe.com. Your internet browser might already have Acrobat® as an extension. The RTF version may be copied into your word processing program, such as Microsoft Word®, and may be customized. Permission is granted to reproduce the figures for educational/training activities. *The copyright line that appears at the bottom of each figure <u>must</u> appear on all reproduced figures.* See installation instructions on the diskette label.

Table

ABOUT THE AUTHORS

Dale Brethower is a professor of psychology at Western Michigan University, with degrees from the University of Kansas (A.B.), Harvard University (A.M.), and the University of Michigan (Ph.D.). He teaches courses in training and development, performance management, and behavioral systems analysis. He has been a consultant for more than thirty years, with a client list including more than sixty public and private sector organizations, primarily in the United States. He has served on advisory boards for the Institute for Rational Living and for Ronningen Research and Development. He is a board member of Triad Performance Technologies and the International Society for Performance Improvement. He is the recipient of a lifetime achievement award in organizational behavior management from the International Association for Behavior Analysis.

Karolyn Smalley, a performance and instructional systems consultant, helps improve performance at the organizational, process, and job levels. She specializes in process improvement projects, performance management systems, and instructional systems. Prior to working as a consultant, Karolyn managed the human resource development department for an organization having more than $7 billion in annual sales. She was able to convert a conventional training department into one that specialized in performance improvement consulting. She is a graduate of Michigan State University, the programmed learning workshop of the University of Michigan, and the M.A. program in industrial/organizational psychology at Western Michigan University.

INDEX

The International Society for Performance Improvement

The International Society for Performance Improvement (ISPI) is the leading international association dedicated to improving productivity and performance in the workplace. Founded in 1962, ISPI represents over ten thousand members throughout the United States and Canada and in nearly forty other countries. ISPI members work in over three thousand businesses, governmental agencies, academic institutions, and other organizations. Monthly meetings of over sixty different chapters provide professional development, services, and information exchange.

ISPI members include performance technologists, training directors, human resource managers, instructional technologists, human factors practitioners, and organizational development consultants. They are business executives, professors, line managers, government leaders, and military commanders. They work in a variety of areas: the armed forces, financial services, government agencies, health services, high technology, manufacturing, telecommunications, travel and hospitality, and universities. ISPI members are leaders in their fields and work settings. They are strategy-oriented, quality-focused, and results-centered.

The mission of ISPI is to improve the performance of individuals and organizations through the application of Human Performance Technology (HPT). ISPI's vision for itself is to be the preferred source of information, education, and advocacy for enhancing individual and organizational effectiveness, and to be respected for the tangible and enduring impact it is having on people, organizations, and the field of performance technology.

ISPI makes a difference to people by helping them grow into skilled professionals who use integrated and systematic approaches to add value to their organizations and the profession. Whether designing training programs, building selection or incentive systems, assisting organizations in their own redesign, or performing myriad other interventions, ISPI members produce results.

ISPI makes a difference to organizations by increasing professional competence and confidence. ISPI members help organizations anticipate opportunities and challenges and develop powerful solutions that contribute to productivity and satisfaction.

ISPI makes a difference to the field of performance technology by expanding the boundaries of what we know about defining, teaching, supporting, and maintaining skilled human performance. With a healthy respect for research and development, a variety of technologies, and collegial interaction, ISPI members use approaches and systems that ensure improved productivity and a better world.

For additional information, contact:

The International Society for Performance Improvement
1300 L Street, N.W., Suite 1250
Washington, DC 20005
Telephone: (202) 408–7969
Fax: (202) 408–7972